Starting you

LAUNCH YOUR OWN SMALL/START UP BUSINESS and IMPROVE YOUR ENTREPRENEURSHIP SKILLS. A USEFUL MARKETING ORIENTED BASED GUIDE | CASE STUDY INCLUDED

Umberto Ferrario

© Copyright 2024 by Umberto Ferrario - All rights reserved.

The following Book is reproduced below with the goal of providing information that is as accurate and reliable as possible. Regardless, purchasing this Book can be seen as consent to the fact that both the publisher and the author of this book are in no way experts on the topics discussed within and that any recommendations or suggestions that are made herein are for entertainment purposes only. Professionals should be consulted as needed prior to undertaking any of the action endorsed herein.

This declaration is deemed fair and valid by both the American Bar Association and the Committee of Publishers Association and is legally binding throughout the United States.

Furthermore, the transmission, duplication, or reproduction of any of the following work including specific information will be considered an illegal act irrespective of if it is done electronically or in print. This extends to creating a secondary or tertiary copy of the work or a recorded copy and is only allowed with the express written consent from the Publisher. All additional right reserved.

The information in the following pages is broadly considered a truthful and accurate account of facts and as such, any inattention, use, or misuse of the information in question by the reader will render any resulting actions solely under their purview. There are no scenarios in which the publisher or the original author of this work can be in any fashion deemed liable for any hardship or damages that may befall them after undertaking information described herein.

Additionally, the information in the following pages is intended only for informational purposes and should thus be thought of as universal. As befitting its nature, it is presented without assurance regarding its prolonged validity or interim quality. Trademarks that are mentioned are done without written consent and can in no way be considered an endorsement from the trademark holder.

CHAPTER 1: WHAT IS A BUSINESS IDEA 6

- Definition of a Business Idea 6
- Profitable Business Idea 11
- Why Having a Clear Business Idea is Important 13
- Example for Us: Enjoying the Benefits and Pleasure of Practicing Sports 16

CHAPTER 2: WHY HAVE A STRATEGIC VISION 19

- Definition of Strategic Vision 21
- Forward-Thinking, Bold & Strong Strategic Vision 23
- Example for Us: Move People Through the Wonders of Sports 25

CHAPTER 3: HOW TO CREATE A LONG-TERM CORPORATE MISSION 27

- Definition of Corporate Mission 29
- Why It's Important to Have a Coherent Corporate Mission 31
- Coherence with the Strategic Vision 33
- Example for Us: Production, Marketing, and Distribution of Products, Articles, and Services for Indoor and Outdoor Sports 37
- Defining Clear Objectives for the Corporate Mission 39
- What are Strategic Objectives 41
- Why It's Better to Define Them in a Business Plan 44
- Coherence with the Company's Strategy and Vision 47

CHAPTER 4: CREATING ACTION PLANS COHERENT WITH THE STRATEGIC VISION 50

- What are Strategic Action Plans 52
- Why You Should Set Action Plans and Responsibilities 54
- Creating an Organizational Chart by Function, Division, Product, or Target Market 57

CHAPTER 5: WRITING A DESCRIPTION OF THE BUSINESS OR ENTREPRENEURIAL ACTIVITY 60

- Definition of Entrepreneur (According to Civil Code) 62
- Definition of Business (According to Civil Code) 64
- Through the Practice of Writing, Stimulating a Virtuous Cycle for Business Plan Development 67
- Clarity of Business Ideas and Plans 69
- Definition of Activities 71
- "Who Does What" Approach to Include in the Company Description 73

CHAPTER 6: CONDUCTING A MARKET ANALYSIS USING APPROPRIATE TOOLS .. 76

- SWOT Analysis 77
- Porter's Model Analysis 79
- Boston Consulting Group Matrix Analysis 81

CHAPTER 7: LISTING YOUR PRODUCTS & SERVICES 83

FROM THE BUSINESS IDEA TO WRITING THE KEY PRODUCTS TO LAUNCH OR REPOSITION IN THE MARKET(S) 84
FROM DEFINING THE STRATEGY TO WRITING THE KEY SERVICES TO LAUNCH OR REMODEL IN THE MARKET(S) 86

CHAPTER 8: DEFINING A MARKETING PLAN 89

CONDUCTING A MARKETING MIX ANALYSIS 90
4PS ANALYSIS: PRODUCT, PRICE, PROMOTION, AND PRODUCT DISTRIBUTION 92
BOSTON CONSULTING GROUP MATRIX ANALYSIS ON PRODUCT/SERVICE LIFE CYCLE STAGES AND TARGET MARKET(S) 95

CHAPTER 9: CONDUCTING CUSTOMER SEGMENTATION 98

BY PRODUCT 99
BY SERVICE 100
BY CUSTOMER TYPE 102
BY GEOGRAPHIC DISTRIBUTION 104

CHAPTER 10: DEVELOPING A LOGISTICS AND OPERATIONS PLAN 106

WHAT IS A LOGISTICS PLAN? 107
WHY HAVE A LOGISTICS PLAN? 108
WHAT IS AN OPERATIONS PLAN? 110
WRITING AN OPERATIONS PLAN IN ACTIONS AND TASKS 111

CHAPTER 11: CREATING A PROFITABLE FINANCIAL PLAN 113

PROPER PREPARATION OF THE FINANCIAL STATEMENTS 114
THE INCOME STATEMENT, THE BALANCE SHEET, AND CALCULATION OF PROFIT OR LOSS 116
RECLASSIFICATION OF THE FINANCIAL STATEMENTS INTO KEY PERFORMANCE INDICATORS . 118
DEFINITION OF ACCOUNTING PRINCIPLES: PROFITABILITY, SOLVENCY, LIQUIDITY 120
WHAT IS A FINANCIAL PLAN 122
WHY YOU NEED A FINANCIAL PLAN 123

CHAPTER 12: DEFINING THE MANAGEMENT ORGANIZATIONAL STRUCTURE (ORGANIZATIONAL CHART) 125

DESIGNING AN ORGANIZATIONAL CHART 126
WHO DOES WHAT 128
WHEN AND WHERE 130
WITH WHOM 131
WHICH RESPONSIBILITIES TO ASSIGN TO THE TEAM / HIERARCHY 132

CHAPTER 13: FINAL DRAFT OF A BUSINESS PLAN FOR POTENTIAL THIRD-PARTY INVESTORS 134

HOW TO CREATE A FINANCIAL PLAN PRESENTATION 134

Why You Need a Financial Plan Presentation 139

CHAPTER 14: MONITORING KEY FINANCIAL INDICATORS 143

From Proper Preparation of the Financial Statements to Reclassification into Consistent Financial Indicators for Making Informed Managerial and Entrepreneurial Decisions 144
The Company's Financial Statements: Income Statement and Balance Sheet 146
Reclassification of Financial Statements into Indicators: ROS / ROI / ROE to Help Understand the Company's Economic and Financial Performance 148
Monitoring Profitability, Solvency, and Liquidity 150
To Gain Deep Insights and Make the Best Strategic Decisions for the Future of the Business 152
To Establish Credibility with Third-Party Investors 155

CHAPTER 15: CASH FLOW ANALYSIS 157

Liquidity Index Generated by the Business Activity 158
Proper Management of Cash Flows 159
Management of Cash Inflows 161
Management of Cash Outflows 162

BONUS CHAPTER: CASE STUDY: LUXOR INCORPORATION LIMITED LIABILITY COMPANYCOMPANY FOUNDERS: 4 PERSONS 165

Vision: Taking Care of People's Eyes Around the World 167
Mission: E-commerce Platform to Sell High-Quality Sunglasses and Eyeglass Frames in the Mid-to-High Price Range 169
A Global Vision for Eye Care and Fashion 171
Market Supply Analysis (Potential and Actual Competitors) 174
Financial Plan: Drafting the Income Statement and Balance Sheet (to Determine Profit and/or Loss) and Reclassification into Key Performance Indicators (to Monitor Profitability, Solvency, Liquidity) 176
Financial Plan Presentation to Third-Party Funders 178
Supplier Analysis and Product Selection (for Us: 3 Sunglasses Lines and 3 Types of Eyeglass Frames for Men and the Same for Women) 180
Pricing Model 183
Mark-Up 184
Marketing Plan (Online Advertising) and Social Media Channels 185

Chapter 1: What is a Business Idea

Definition of a Business Idea

A **business idea** is the cornerstone of any entrepreneurial venture. It represents the initial concept or vision that inspires the creation of a product, service, or solution aimed at addressing a particular problem or fulfilling a need in the marketplace. In essence, it is the seed from which a business grows, shaping the direction, structure, and potential success of the enterprise. A well-defined business idea is not just about having an exciting notion; it must be grounded in practicality and geared toward profitability.

At its core, a business idea is a solution. It identifies a gap in the market—a problem, a desire, or an unmet need—and presents a new way of filling it. This solution could involve offering a new product, improving upon an existing service, or innovating how certain tasks are performed. However, to be more than just an abstract thought, a business idea must be accompanied by a clear understanding of the potential target market, the demand for the proposed product or service, and how it can be delivered in a way that is both cost-effective and sustainable.

Defining a business idea requires a deep dive into various factors that influence its viability. First and foremost, the entrepreneur must understand the nature of the problem their idea is addressing. Is it something that many people experience? Does it have the potential to improve the quality of life, productivity, or satisfaction of its users? These questions help in refining the idea, ensuring it is relevant and capable of capturing the interest of potential customers.

A business idea is also the starting point for defining your competitive advantage. This is what differentiates your business from others in the market. Whether through innovative features, better pricing, exceptional customer service, or a novel distribution method, the idea should provide something unique that will draw customers away from competitors and toward your solution.

In addition to being relevant and unique, a successful business idea must be **profitable**. It's not enough to simply solve a problem or introduce something new; the idea must generate revenue. Profitability depends on several factors, including cost management, market size, pricing strategy, and the scalability of the business. Entrepreneurs must assess whether their idea can be monetized effectively—whether through direct sales, subscription models, or other revenue-generating approaches. They also need to evaluate whether the potential profits justify the initial investment and the risk involved in starting the business.

Profitable Business Idea

Not every idea, no matter how creative or unique, has the potential to become a profitable business. A **profitable business idea** is one that can be transformed into a sustainable venture, generating more revenue than the costs required to operate it. This requires careful consideration of factors such as market demand, competition, and operational expenses.

To develop a profitable business idea, it is essential to conduct thorough market research. This includes identifying the target audience, understanding their needs and preferences, and evaluating whether there is sufficient demand for the product or service being offered. Entrepreneurs must ask themselves: How large is the potential customer base? Are there enough people willing to pay for the solution being provided? Is the market growing, stable, or declining? The answers to these questions will help determine the financial viability of the idea.

Another critical aspect of profitability is **scalability**. A scalable business idea is one that can grow and expand without a proportionate increase in costs. For example, a software-based business may require significant upfront investment in development, but once the product is created, it can be sold to an unlimited number of customers without a corresponding rise in production costs. On the other hand, a business that relies heavily on manual labor or high production costs may struggle to scale and maintain profitability over time. Entrepreneurs must consider whether their idea can be scaled and how quickly it can grow.

Profitability also depends on pricing strategy. Setting the right price for your product or service is crucial for maximizing revenue while remaining competitive. Pricing must reflect both the value provided to customers and the costs incurred by the business. If prices are set too low, the business may struggle to cover its expenses and turn a profit. If prices are too high, customers may choose to go elsewhere. Striking the right balance is key to ensuring that the business remains profitable in the long term.

Lastly, a profitable business idea must be **sustainable**. This means that the business can operate and generate revenue consistently over time, without being overly reliant on external factors such as short-term trends or one-time sales. A sustainable business is built on a solid foundation of repeat customers, efficient operations, and strong brand loyalty. This requires ongoing market analysis, a commitment to quality, and adaptability to changing market conditions.

Why Having a Clear Business Idea is Important

Having a clear and well-defined business idea is essential for several reasons. First, it provides **direction**. When entrepreneurs have a clear idea of what they want to achieve and how they plan to achieve it, they are better equipped to make informed decisions about product development, marketing strategies, and operational plans. Clarity of purpose ensures that every aspect of the business is aligned with the overall goal, reducing the risk of missteps or wasted resources.

Second, a clear business idea helps to attract **investors and partners**. Investors want to see that the entrepreneur has a solid plan and a well-thought-out strategy for turning their idea into a successful business. A vague or poorly defined idea will struggle to gain traction with investors, while a clear and compelling vision can inspire confidence and secure funding.

Finally, a clear business idea serves as the foundation for the **business plan**, which is essential for guiding the business through its growth stages. A well-defined idea allows entrepreneurs to develop specific goals, create detailed action plans, and track progress over time.

Profitable Business Idea

A **profitable business idea** is the backbone of any successful enterprise. It goes beyond the excitement of an initial concept, demanding careful evaluation to ensure that the idea can generate consistent revenue while covering its costs. Not every business idea, no matter how creative or innovative, will necessarily lead to profitability. To determine if an idea has the potential to be profitable, several key factors must be considered, including market demand, operational costs, pricing strategies, and scalability.

First and foremost, **market demand** is a crucial determinant of profitability. A business idea must address a real need or solve a problem that a significant number of people are willing to pay for. Market research plays a vital role in understanding the target audience, their preferences, and the size of the potential customer base. If the demand for the product or service is too small or too niche, the business may struggle to reach a large enough market to sustain its operations. Conversely, a high-demand product or service can lead to steady sales and long-term profitability.

Another critical factor is the **cost structure** of the business. Even if there is substantial demand, the costs involved in producing, marketing, and delivering the product or service must be carefully managed. A profitable business idea must have a sound balance between revenue generation and cost control. Entrepreneurs need to assess their fixed and variable costs, such as materials, labor, marketing, and overhead, and ensure that the pricing of their product or service allows for a healthy profit margin after these expenses are covered.

Pricing strategy is closely linked to profitability. Pricing too low might attract more customers initially, but it could undermine the business's ability to cover costs and achieve profitability. On the other hand, setting prices too high may discourage potential customers and limit market penetration. The right pricing strategy should reflect the value offered to customers while also ensuring a sufficient margin for the business to thrive. This balance requires an in-depth understanding of competitors' pricing, customer willingness to pay, and the overall value proposition of the business.

Lastly, **scalability** is a significant driver of profitability. A scalable business is one that can grow its revenue without a proportional increase in costs. For example, digital products or online services can often scale more easily than physical products, as they can be replicated or delivered to a wider audience with minimal additional costs. The ability to scale allows businesses to reach new markets and increase profitability over time.

In conclusion, a profitable business idea requires careful consideration of demand, costs, pricing, and scalability. These factors, when aligned, create a solid foundation for building a business that can generate sustainable profits.

Why Having a Clear Business Idea is Important

A **clear business idea** is essential for the success of any entrepreneurial venture. It serves as the guiding force behind all strategic decisions, from product development to marketing and operations. A vague or poorly defined business idea can lead to confusion, misaligned goals, and inefficient use of resources, ultimately increasing the risk of failure. On the other hand, a well-defined and focused business idea provides a roadmap for the entrepreneur, ensuring that every aspect of the business aligns with its core vision and objectives. Understanding why a clear business idea is important can significantly improve your chances of building a successful and sustainable business.

One of the primary reasons why clarity is crucial is that it provides **direction**. When you have a well-defined business idea, you know exactly what your business stands for, what it offers, and who it serves. This clear sense of purpose allows you to make informed decisions that are consistent with your overall vision. For instance, when deciding on the features of a new product or the services you want to provide, having a clear business idea ensures that you remain focused on your target audience's needs. It helps you avoid distractions, such as pursuing unrelated opportunities that might seem profitable in the short term but detract from your long-term goals. Essentially, clarity enables you to remain true to your core mission, ensuring that all business activities are aligned and coherent.

In addition to providing direction, a clear business idea is critical for **resource allocation**. Every business operates with limited resources, whether it be time, money, or manpower. With a clear business idea, you can allocate these resources more effectively. When you understand exactly what your business is about, you can focus your efforts on the areas that will have the most significant impact. This means that you can prioritize investments in product development, marketing strategies, or customer service initiatives that are in line with your business's core objectives. Without a clear business idea, you risk spreading your resources too thin, investing in areas that don't contribute to the overall success of the business. Moreover, a clear business idea enhances your ability to **attract investors, partners, and employees**. Investors, in particular, want to see that you have a well-thought-out plan and a clear understanding of your business's purpose and potential. A vague or unfocused business idea is unlikely to inspire confidence among potential investors, making it difficult to secure funding. On the other hand, a clear and compelling business idea demonstrates that you have thoroughly considered your market, your competition, and your strategy for achieving profitability. This clarity not only attracts investors but also makes it easier to bring on partners and employees who share your vision and are committed to helping you achieve your business goals.

A well-defined business idea also simplifies the process of **communicating with your target audience**. In today's crowded marketplace, businesses must clearly differentiate themselves from their competitors to attract and retain customers. A vague or inconsistent message can confuse potential customers and dilute your brand's impact. When your business idea is clear, it becomes much easier to craft a compelling value proposition that resonates with your target market. This clarity allows you to communicate your business's unique strengths and benefits effectively, helping you stand out from competitors and build a loyal customer base.

Finally, a clear business idea serves as the foundation for your **business plan**. A business plan is essential for guiding your business through its various stages of growth, from initial startup to long-term sustainability. The clearer your business idea, the easier it is to develop specific goals, create actionable strategies, and measure your progress over time. A business plan based on a strong, clear idea gives you a practical tool for navigating challenges and seizing opportunities as they arise.

Example for Us: Enjoying the Benefits and Pleasure of Practicing Sports

A clear business idea not only defines the product or service being offered but also illustrates how it can positively impact the lives of its target audience. To better understand how a clear and well-defined idea translates into a successful venture, let's consider an example rooted in the world of sports. This example shows how a simple yet powerful concept—encouraging people to enjoy the benefits and pleasures of practicing sports—can serve as the foundation for a profitable and impactful business.

The Concept: Imagine that the core idea of the business is to promote an active lifestyle by making sports more accessible, enjoyable, and rewarding for people of all ages and fitness levels. The primary goal of this business is to inspire individuals to integrate physical activity into their daily routines, highlighting the mental, physical, and social benefits that come with regular exercise. From reducing stress and improving mental clarity to fostering a sense of community through team sports, this business idea taps into a growing societal trend focused on health and wellness.

By offering products and services that encourage physical activity, the business has a clear value proposition: helping people achieve healthier, more active lifestyles while also enjoying the pleasure that sports bring. The key here is to combine the physical benefits of sports with the emotional rewards that come from pursuing personal goals, building friendships, and enhancing overall well-being.

Target Market: The business idea is designed to appeal to a broad audience, including children, adults, and seniors. It aims to serve individuals who are passionate about fitness, as well as those who may be new to sports or looking for fun, accessible ways to stay active. This flexibility allows the business to attract a diverse range of customers, from serious athletes to casual enthusiasts and families seeking recreational activities. The market for health and fitness is vast, and by focusing on the joy and benefits of sports, this business can carve out a unique niche.

Products and Services: To bring this idea to life, the business offers a variety of products and services aimed at making sports participation more accessible and enjoyable. These offerings could include:

- **Sports equipment**: High-quality gear designed for ease of use and enjoyment, catering to beginners and seasoned athletes alike.
- **Fitness classes and workshops**: Fun, engaging group activities that focus on different sports, from team sports like soccer and basketball to individual activities like yoga, running, or cycling.
- **Sports-themed events and community challenges**: Organizing local tournaments, charity runs, and fitness challenges to bring people together and foster a sense of community around sports.

Additionally, the business can offer online resources, such as fitness tutorials, workout plans, and tips for staying motivated. The idea is to create an ecosystem where people can easily find the tools and inspiration they need to engage in sports, regardless of their skill level or experience.

Marketing the Benefits: The marketing strategy for this business would center around the tangible and intangible benefits of practicing sports. Campaigns would emphasize not only the physical health benefits, such as weight loss, muscle strengthening, and cardiovascular improvement, but also the emotional and social rewards. Testimonials from customers who have improved their quality of life through sports could be featured, alongside messages that highlight the sheer fun and enjoyment of being active.

Brand Identity: The business would position itself as a brand that advocates for a balanced lifestyle, where fitness is not a chore but a source of joy. The branding would focus on creating an inclusive community where everyone, regardless of their fitness level, is encouraged to participate in sports and experience the benefits. By fostering a positive, welcoming environment, the business would attract a loyal customer base that sees sports not only as a way to stay fit but also as an essential part of their lives.

Scalability and Profitability: This business idea has strong potential for scalability. As the interest in health and fitness continues to grow, expanding the range of products and services, opening new locations, and offering online memberships or fitness programs would allow the business to reach new markets. Additionally, partnerships with local schools, gyms, and sports leagues could help broaden its influence and reach. With the right pricing strategy, it can be profitable while still being affordable to a wide range of customers.

Chapter 2: Why Have a Strategic Vision

Why Have a Strategic Vision
A **strategic vision** is essential for the long-term success and sustainability of any business. It serves as a guiding light, helping entrepreneurs and business leaders stay focused on their ultimate goals while navigating the challenges and opportunities that arise along the way. Without a clear strategic vision, businesses may find themselves lost, making short-term decisions that don't align with their overall purpose or values. The importance of a strategic vision cannot be overstated, as it not only provides direction but also inspires and motivates everyone involved in the organization.

A strategic vision defines where the business aims to go in the future. It outlines the long-term objectives and aspirations, providing a framework for decision-making at all levels of the organization. This vision acts as a roadmap, allowing the business to stay on course even when market conditions change or unexpected obstacles emerge. With a clear vision in place, businesses can adapt to these challenges without losing sight of their ultimate goals. This ability to remain focused and adaptable is critical in today's fast-paced, competitive marketplace.

Additionally, having a strategic vision helps businesses make better **resource allocation** decisions. When you understand where you want your business to go, you can prioritize investments and initiatives that align with this vision. This means focusing on the areas that will drive growth and long-term success, rather than getting distracted by short-term gains or opportunities that may not support the overall strategy. By aligning resources with the strategic vision, businesses can ensure that they are working toward their most important objectives.

A strategic vision also plays a key role in **building organizational culture**. It defines the core values and principles that guide how the business operates, both internally and externally. When employees and stakeholders understand the business's long-term vision, they are more likely to feel connected to the mission and motivated to contribute to its success. This sense of purpose can boost morale, foster collaboration, and create a strong organizational culture that supports innovation and growth.

Moreover, a well-defined strategic vision enhances a business's ability to **communicate its goals and objectives** to external stakeholders, including investors, partners, and customers. Investors, in particular, are more likely to support businesses that have a clear vision for the future, as it demonstrates that the leadership has a long-term plan and understands the steps needed to achieve it. Customers, too, are drawn to businesses that have a compelling vision, as it shows commitment and direction, helping to build trust and loyalty.

Definition of Strategic Vision

A **strategic vision** is a clear and compelling statement that defines the long-term goals and aspirations of a business. It outlines where the organization wants to be in the future and provides a roadmap for achieving those objectives. Unlike a mission statement, which focuses on the company's current purpose and operations, a strategic vision is forward-looking, describing what the business aims to become over time. It is a critical element of strategic planning, as it sets the direction for all future decisions and actions.

At its core, a strategic vision answers the question: **"Where do we want to go?"** It reflects the leadership's ambitions for the business and serves as a guide for making important choices about growth, innovation, and market positioning. The vision must be bold yet achievable, providing a sense of purpose and direction while also being grounded in the realities of the business environment. A strong strategic vision is both inspiring and practical, offering a clear path forward while motivating employees, investors, and stakeholders to work toward common goals.

A well-crafted strategic vision typically includes several key components:

- **Long-term goals**: These are the high-level objectives that the business aims to achieve over a specific period, usually 5 to 10 years or longer. These goals might include market leadership, global expansion, product innovation, or revenue milestones.

- **Core values**: The strategic vision often incorporates the values and principles that guide the business's operations. These values help shape the company culture and define how the business interacts with its customers, employees, and the broader community.
- **Aspirational elements**: A strategic vision should inspire and motivate. It should describe a future state that is compelling and desirable, one that encourages employees to strive for excellence and pushes the business to innovate and grow.
- **Competitive positioning**: The vision should also include a sense of how the business intends to differentiate itself from competitors. This could involve becoming a leader in quality, customer service, innovation, or social responsibility.

For example, a strategic vision for a tech company might state: "Our vision is to become the world leader in sustainable technology solutions, delivering innovative products that reduce environmental impact while enhancing the quality of life for millions of people worldwide." This vision provides a clear sense of direction, motivating the company to focus on sustainability, innovation, and global impact.

In essence, a strategic vision is about setting a course for the future. It is not just about where the business is today, but where it wants to be and how it plans to get there. This long-term perspective helps the business navigate challenges, seize opportunities, and stay focused on its ultimate goals. A well-defined strategic vision is a powerful tool for shaping a successful, sustainable business.

Forward-Thinking, Bold & Strong Strategic Vision

A **forward-thinking, bold, and strong strategic vision** is one that pushes the boundaries of what a business can achieve. It goes beyond incremental improvements or short-term gains, aiming for transformative change that positions the company as a leader in its field. Such a vision challenges conventional thinking, encouraging innovation and risk-taking while setting the business on a path toward significant growth and success.

Being forward-thinking means anticipating future trends and preparing the business to capitalize on them. This involves staying ahead of technological advancements, market shifts, and evolving customer preferences. A business with a forward-thinking strategic vision doesn't just react to changes in the market; it proactively shapes the future of its industry. For example, a company in the renewable energy sector might develop a vision that emphasizes pioneering new technologies to combat climate change, positioning itself as a leader in the green energy revolution.

A bold strategic vision is one that dares to aim high. It sets ambitious goals that challenge the business to stretch beyond its current capabilities. Bold visions often involve significant innovation or disruption, changing the way an industry operates or introducing entirely new ways of doing business. However, a bold vision must also be grounded in reality. While it should inspire ambition, it must be achievable with the right resources, strategies, and commitment. A balance between aspiration and feasibility is key to ensuring that the vision can be realized.

A strong strategic vision, on the other hand, is one that resonates deeply with both internal and external stakeholders. It aligns with the business's core values and creates a sense of purpose that motivates employees and builds loyalty among customers. A strong vision is not just about financial success; it also reflects the company's commitment to making a positive impact on society, whether through innovation, sustainability, or social responsibility. Together, these elements create a strategic vision that is both ambitious and achievable, inspiring the business to innovate, grow, and lead. A forward-thinking, bold, and strong vision can transform a business, setting it on a path toward long-term success and sustainability.

Example for Us: Move People Through the Wonders of Sports

Sports have the unique power to inspire, motivate, and transform people, making them a universal language that transcends borders and cultures. The mission to **move people through the wonders of sports** reflects the profound impact that physical activity and athleticism can have on individuals and society as a whole. Whether it's the thrill of competition, the joy of personal achievement, or the sense of community that sports foster, the influence of sports extends far beyond physical fitness—it touches mental well-being, personal growth, and social cohesion.
For a business rooted in sports, like a company selling sports equipment, apparel, or even providing sports-related services, this mission captures the essence of what it means to engage customers in a lifestyle centered around movement, health, and exploration. The idea is not just to sell products but to promote an active way of life, where individuals of all backgrounds can experience the benefits of physical activity, whether they are seasoned athletes or beginners.
Engaging Customers Beyond Products
When a company adopts a mission to move people through sports, it goes beyond simply offering products—it becomes about creating **experiences** and **communities** around those products. For instance, a company might host sports events, workshops, or training sessions that bring people together to enjoy the pleasures of physical activity. These events not only promote health but also allow participants to bond with others who share similar passions, building a sense of belonging and support.

Additionally, a business focused on sports can inspire people through **storytelling**, sharing stories of athletes, adventurers, and everyday individuals who have transformed their lives through sports. By highlighting the personal journeys of success, perseverance, and growth, the company can connect with its customers on a deeper level, fostering loyalty and emotional engagement. For example, profiles of athletes who have overcome adversity to achieve their goals can motivate customers to pursue their own dreams, whether through sport or in other areas of life.

Promoting Accessibility and Inclusivity

A key aspect of moving people through the wonders of sports is ensuring that **sports are accessible** to everyone, regardless of age, skill level, or financial background. This mission might involve developing products that cater to a wide range of abilities, from professional-grade equipment for athletes to beginner-friendly items for those just starting their sports journey. Offering inclusive products not only broadens the customer base but also reinforces the company's commitment to making sports an enriching experience for all.

Moreover, inclusivity can be extended through **community outreach programs**, where the company sponsors local sports teams, donates equipment to underserved communities, or provides scholarships to young athletes. These initiatives demonstrate that the company's mission is not just profit-driven but focused on making a positive social impact, encouraging individuals who may not otherwise have access to sports to get involved.

Inspiring a Lifelong Love of Movement

By promoting sports as an ongoing journey of discovery and growth, the company encourages customers to adopt an active lifestyle, not just for a short period but for life. This could involve promoting sports as a form of **mental and emotional wellness**, highlighting the therapeutic benefits of movement, such as stress relief, improved mood, and enhanced focus. For many, sports become a way to break free from daily stresses, providing an outlet for energy, creativity, and reflection.

In this way, moving people through sports also means inspiring a lifelong passion for physical activity. It encourages individuals to challenge themselves, set new goals, and explore different sports over time, from running marathons to hiking, swimming, or team sports. By fostering this mindset, the company not only keeps customers engaged with its products but also nurtures a community of people who are constantly striving to improve themselves and explore new possibilities through sports.

Chapter 3: How to Create a Long-Term Corporate Mission

How to Create a Long-Term Corporate Mission
Creating a **long-term corporate mission** is one of the most critical steps in establishing a successful and sustainable business. The corporate mission defines the company's overarching purpose, outlining why it exists and what it seeks to achieve in the long term. Unlike a business strategy, which may evolve over time, the mission is typically more stable, reflecting the core values and principles that guide the organization. A well-crafted corporate mission serves as a foundational element of the business, aligning all stakeholders—employees, investors, and customers—around a common goal.

The first step in creating a long-term corporate mission is to identify the fundamental **purpose** of the business. This goes beyond simply describing the products or services offered; it encompasses the broader impact the company wants to have on its customers, community, or even the world. For example, a technology company might have the purpose of improving people's lives through innovation, while a sustainable food business might aim to promote healthier eating habits and protect the environment. The mission should capture the essence of the business's role in society and what it ultimately strives to accomplish.

Once the purpose is clear, the next step is to incorporate the **core values** that define how the business will achieve its goals. These values should reflect the ethical principles and cultural norms that guide decision-making within the company. For instance, a company that values customer service might commit to prioritizing customer satisfaction in every aspect of its operations. Another business might emphasize environmental sustainability, making it a central focus in its supply chain and product development processes. Core values help establish the moral framework that will influence all aspects of the business, from strategic decisions to daily operations.

Finally, the corporate mission should be **aspirational yet achievable**. It must inspire both employees and external stakeholders while remaining grounded in the company's capabilities and market environment. A mission that is too vague or overly ambitious can feel disconnected from the actual work being done, while one that is too narrow may fail to inspire or excite. Striking the right balance between ambition and realism ensures that the mission not only guides the business but also motivates everyone involved to work towards a common goal.

In conclusion, creating a long-term corporate mission requires clarity of purpose, strong alignment with core values, and a realistic yet aspirational vision for the future. A well-defined mission acts as a compass for the organization, helping it stay true to its objectives and guiding it through challenges and opportunities alike.

Definition of Corporate Mission

A **corporate mission** is a formal statement that defines a company's purpose, core values, and primary goals. It articulates why the company exists, what it aims to achieve, and how it plans to accomplish those objectives. While a corporate vision focuses on where the company wants to go in the future, the mission is more grounded in the present, serving as a guide for day-to-day operations and decision-making.

At its core, the corporate mission addresses several key elements:

- **Purpose**: The mission should clearly state the reason for the company's existence beyond just making a profit. It answers the fundamental question of why the business was created and what societal need or problem it aims to solve. For example, a healthcare company's mission might be to improve access to quality care for underserved communities, while an educational institution might focus on empowering students through innovative learning experiences.

- **Core Values**: The mission should incorporate the values that define the company's ethical and cultural framework. These values represent the guiding principles that influence how the business operates and interacts with its customers, employees, and the broader community. Values such as integrity, innovation, or customer focus help shape the company's identity and decision-making processes.
- **Primary Goals**: The mission should outline the company's long-term objectives. These goals are broader and more enduring than specific business strategies or financial targets. They reflect the company's aspirations for making a meaningful impact in its industry or on society as a whole. For example, a renewable energy company might aim to lead the transition to clean energy by providing sustainable alternatives to fossil fuels.

A corporate mission is often concise yet impactful, distilling the essence of the company into a few powerful sentences. It should be clear enough to guide daily operations but broad enough to encompass future growth and evolution. A strong corporate mission not only helps align internal stakeholders—such as employees and management—but also communicates the company's purpose and values to external audiences, including customers, investors, and partners.

For example, consider the mission of a tech company focused on accessibility: "To leverage technology to create products that empower people with disabilities, improving their quality of life and fostering independence." This mission is clear and purposeful, reflecting the company's dedication to a specific cause while also allowing for future innovation and growth within that space.

In summary, a corporate mission is a fundamental statement that defines what a company stands for, what it aims to achieve, and the values that guide its journey. It is a powerful tool for aligning the organization's efforts, providing a sense of purpose, and communicating its identity to the world.

Why It's Important to Have a Coherent Corporate Mission

Having a **coherent corporate mission** is crucial for the success of any business. A coherent mission is one that is consistent with the company's goals, values, and long-term vision. It acts as a unifying force within the organization, aligning employees, leadership, and external stakeholders around a shared purpose. Without coherence, the mission risks becoming fragmented, disconnected from the actual work being done, and less effective in driving the company toward its objectives.

One of the primary reasons coherence is important is that it ensures **consistency** across all aspects of the business. From marketing and branding to product development and customer service, a coherent mission provides a stable foundation that informs all decisions and actions. This consistency helps the company maintain a strong and recognizable identity in the marketplace, fostering trust and loyalty among customers. When a company's mission is coherent and well-aligned with its operations, it creates a seamless experience for customers and stakeholders, reinforcing the company's values and purpose.

A coherent corporate mission also plays a key role in **employee engagement**. When employees understand and connect with the company's mission, they are more likely to feel motivated and invested in their work. This sense of purpose can enhance job satisfaction and productivity, as employees see how their efforts contribute to the larger goals of the organization. A coherent mission helps create a strong organizational culture, where everyone is working toward the same objectives, leading to improved collaboration, innovation, and overall performance.
Moreover, coherence in the corporate mission is essential for **long-term planning**. A mission that aligns with the company's strategic vision ensures that short-term actions are in harmony with long-term goals. This alignment allows the business to grow and adapt while staying true to its core values and purpose. In times of change or uncertainty, a coherent mission provides a stable point of reference, helping the company navigate challenges without losing sight of its overarching objectives.
In conclusion, a coherent corporate mission is vital for maintaining consistency, enhancing employee engagement, and ensuring long-term success. It acts as a guiding force that aligns the company's efforts and helps it stay focused on its core purpose, even as it grows and evolves.

Coherence with the Strategic Vision

Ensuring **coherence with the strategic vision** is critical to a company's long-term success. The strategic vision provides a high-level roadmap that outlines the company's overarching goals and aspirations, guiding decision-making across every aspect of the business. Maintaining coherence with this vision ensures that all actions, initiatives, and operations align with the core mission, fostering consistency and enabling the company to stay focused on achieving its objectives.

A company's strategic vision serves as its compass, defining where it wants to go and how it plans to get there. Every department, project, and team member plays a role in contributing to this long-term vision, which can range from becoming an industry leader to driving innovation or creating social impact. Ensuring coherence means that all tactical decisions, from product development to marketing strategies, are in harmony with this larger goal. For example, if a company's strategic vision is to be a leader in sustainability, all operational choices—such as sourcing materials, designing products, and implementing production processes—must reflect this commitment to environmental responsibility.

Alignment in Decision-Making

One of the key aspects of maintaining coherence with the strategic vision is ensuring that all **decision-making** processes are aligned with it. Every action taken by the company should support the strategic objectives laid out by leadership. For instance, a company that envisions expanding globally should consistently pursue international growth opportunities and invest in building global partnerships. This alignment ensures that daily operations and long-term strategies reinforce each other, avoiding situations where resources are allocated to activities that detract from the company's ultimate goals.

Without such alignment, companies risk engaging in initiatives that seem beneficial in the short term but deviate from the broader strategic direction, leading to wasted resources or missed opportunities. For example, if a company focused on premium, high-quality products suddenly shifts to offering lower-priced goods to quickly capture a new market, it may dilute its brand identity and alienate its existing customer base. Ensuring coherence with the vision means that even during growth or change, the core values and direction of the company remain intact.

Consistency Across Departments

Coherence with the strategic vision also involves ensuring that **every department** within the organization is working toward the same goals. Each department should have clear objectives that support the company's overall mission. This consistency helps avoid silos where different teams might operate with conflicting priorities. For example, the marketing department might aim to build brand recognition while the sales team focuses on short-term revenue generation. If these teams are not aligned with the strategic vision, they may implement strategies that conflict with one another. Marketing might prioritize long-term brand-building campaigns, while sales may push for aggressive discounting, potentially undermining the brand's premium image.

By fostering cross-departmental communication and ensuring that each team understands how its objectives fit into the larger vision, companies can create a unified approach to achieving success. This coherence ensures that all efforts are pulling in the same direction, making the organization more efficient and effective in its pursuits.

Adaptability While Staying True to the Vision

Achieving coherence with the strategic vision does not mean rigidly sticking to a predetermined plan without adaptation. Markets, technologies, and customer preferences constantly evolve, and businesses must remain flexible to succeed. However, while adaptability is crucial, it should never come at the expense of the core strategic vision. For instance, if a technology company's strategic vision revolves around being an industry innovator, it should adapt to new technological advancements while staying true to its commitment to innovation, rather than merely following market trends.

In this way, coherence with the strategic vision provides a **stable foundation** that allows a business to navigate changes and challenges while maintaining a clear sense of purpose. Adapting operations and strategies to meet current demands can be done without sacrificing the company's core mission and long-term goals.

Example for Us: Production, Marketing, and Distribution of Products, Articles, and Services for Indoor and Outdoor Sports

In the world of sports, businesses can create thriving operations by focusing on the **production, marketing, and distribution of products, articles, and services** tailored for both indoor and outdoor sports. This example demonstrates how a clear and well-structured corporate mission can lead to success by aligning the company's efforts across different areas—from product development to marketing and supply chain logistics.

Imagine a business whose mission is to make sports accessible to everyone, regardless of their environment. The company's focus could be on producing high-quality, durable sports equipment and apparel for a wide range of activities, from team sports like basketball and soccer to individual pursuits like yoga, running, and hiking. Whether customers are playing indoors in a gym or outdoors in a park, the company's product line would be designed to enhance their experience, providing them with the tools they need to engage in their favorite activities with confidence.

The company's corporate mission might state something like: "Our mission is to empower people to lead active, healthy lifestyles by providing top-quality sports equipment, apparel, and services for both indoor and outdoor activities. We strive to inspire everyone, from beginners to seasoned athletes, to enjoy the physical and mental benefits of sports through our innovative, durable, and accessible products."

To fulfill this mission, the company would need to excel in three key areas:

- **Production**: Ensuring the highest standards of quality, functionality, and design in the products it offers. This would involve using cutting-edge materials and production methods to create durable, comfortable, and performance-enhancing gear. The product range might include everything from basketball shoes and yoga mats to mountain bikes and running gear.
- **Marketing**: Effectively promoting these products to a diverse audience, using targeted campaigns that emphasize the benefits of sports participation. The marketing strategy could focus on the emotional appeal of sports—building communities, achieving personal goals, and improving overall health. By leveraging social media, sponsorships, and influencer partnerships, the company could build a strong brand that resonates with active individuals of all ages.
- **Distribution**: Ensuring that products are easily accessible to customers through both physical stores and online platforms. Efficient distribution channels would be crucial for reaching customers wherever they are, whether they prefer shopping in local sports shops or ordering online for home delivery. International expansion could be part of the long-term plan, ensuring the products reach a global market.

By aligning its production, marketing, and distribution strategies with its mission, the company would ensure that all aspects of the business are working toward a common goal. This coherence would enhance customer satisfaction, brand loyalty, and ultimately, the company's profitability. A clear mission, combined with strategic execution, can create a successful and sustainable business in the competitive sports industry.

Defining Clear Objectives for the Corporate Mission

To achieve the goals outlined in a corporate mission, it is essential to **define clear objectives** that provide a roadmap for the company's growth and success. Objectives help to translate the broad vision of the mission into specific, measurable, and actionable steps that guide the company's efforts over time. Without clearly defined objectives, a corporate mission may remain vague and difficult to implement, making it challenging to drive the business forward in a structured and effective manner.

Clear objectives are typically aligned with several key areas of business performance, including **financial goals, operational efficiency, market positioning**, and **customer satisfaction**. These objectives should be realistic, yet ambitious, pushing the company to continuously improve and adapt to the changing needs of its market. For example, a sports equipment company's mission to make sports accessible might translate into objectives like expanding product offerings to include new sports, increasing market share in specific regions, or achieving a certain level of customer satisfaction through improved product design.

One of the key aspects of defining clear objectives is ensuring that they are **SMART**—Specific, Measurable, Achievable, Relevant, and Time-bound. These criteria help ensure that the objectives are not only clear but also feasible within the company's capabilities and resources. Let's break down these elements:

- **Specific**: Objectives should be clear and precise, leaving no room for ambiguity. For instance, instead of a vague objective like "grow the business," a specific objective might be "increase market share in the outdoor sports segment by 15% over the next two years."
- **Measurable**: The objectives must be quantifiable, so the company can track its progress and determine whether it is on track to achieve its goals. This could involve metrics such as sales figures, market share percentages, or customer satisfaction ratings.
- **Achievable**: While objectives should be ambitious, they must also be realistic and attainable given the company's resources and market conditions. Setting overly lofty goals can lead to frustration and disengagement among employees.
- **Relevant**: The objectives should align directly with the company's corporate mission and long-term vision. If an objective doesn't contribute to the overall mission, it may not be worth pursuing.
- **Time-bound**: Every objective should have a clear timeframe for completion, whether it's six months, a year, or five years. Having a deadline creates urgency and helps keep the team focused on achieving the desired outcomes.

Defining clear objectives also involves regular **review and adjustment**. As the company evolves and market conditions change, objectives may need to be refined to ensure they remain relevant and achievable. This flexibility is crucial for ensuring that the corporate mission continues to guide the company toward long-term success, even as it adapts to new opportunities and challenges.

In summary, defining clear objectives is essential for operationalizing the corporate mission. By breaking down the mission into specific, measurable, and achievable goals, businesses can create a focused and structured approach to growth and success, ensuring that every action taken contributes meaningfully to the company's broader vision.

What are Strategic Objectives

Strategic objectives are the high-level goals that an organization sets to achieve its long-term vision and mission. These objectives go beyond day-to-day operations, focusing instead on the broader, more impactful actions that drive sustainable growth and competitive advantage. Strategic objectives are essential for providing direction and purpose to an organization, guiding leadership in making decisions that align with the company's long-term goals. They typically focus on areas such as market expansion, product innovation, financial growth, and organizational development.

The primary purpose of strategic objectives is to **bridge the gap** between the company's current state and its desired future. For example, if a sports company's long-term mission is to become a global leader in the sports equipment industry, its strategic objectives might include expanding into new international markets, developing innovative products that meet emerging consumer needs, or forming strategic partnerships with leading sports brands or influencers. These objectives are designed to propel the company toward its mission in a deliberate, structured manner.

Strategic objectives are usually **multi-faceted** and can be categorized into several areas:
- **Financial objectives**: These focus on the company's profitability, revenue growth, and financial sustainability. For example, a company might set a strategic objective to increase annual revenue by 20% over the next five years, or to improve profit margins by optimizing production processes.
- **Market objectives**: These are aimed at increasing market share, entering new geographical regions, or dominating a particular product category. A strategic market objective could be to become the leading provider of indoor fitness equipment in North America within the next three years.
- **Operational objectives**: These focus on improving the efficiency and effectiveness of the company's internal processes. This might include objectives such as reducing production lead times, improving supply chain management, or enhancing the quality of customer service.
- **Product innovation objectives**: These are aimed at developing new products or improving existing ones to meet evolving consumer needs and preferences. For example, a strategic objective could involve launching a new line of eco-friendly sports gear made from sustainable materials, aligning with both customer demand and environmental responsibility.
- **Employee and organizational development objectives**: These focus on building a strong internal team and culture, ensuring the company has the talent and leadership needed to achieve its long-term goals. Strategic objectives in this area might include improving employee retention, investing in leadership training, or fostering a more inclusive and innovative corporate culture.

Setting strategic objectives requires careful analysis of the **internal and external environment**. Internally, the company must assess its strengths, weaknesses, and resources to determine what is achievable. Externally, it must consider market trends, customer preferences, and the competitive landscape to ensure its objectives are relevant and timely. By taking both internal and external factors into account, businesses can set strategic objectives that are realistic and aligned with their broader mission.

In conclusion, strategic objectives are the high-level goals that guide a company's long-term growth and success. They provide a framework for decision-making and help ensure that the company's efforts are focused on achieving its mission and vision. Strategic objectives are essential for maintaining momentum, driving innovation, and staying competitive in a rapidly evolving marketplace.

Why It's Better to Define Them in a Business Plan

Defining **strategic objectives** within the framework of a **business plan** is a critical step for any organization looking to achieve long-term success. A business plan acts as a comprehensive roadmap for the company's growth, outlining not only the overall vision and mission but also the specific, actionable steps needed to reach those goals. Incorporating strategic objectives into the business plan ensures that these high-level goals are not just theoretical but are grounded in a practical, measurable approach that guides decision-making at every level of the organization.

One key reason why it is better to define strategic objectives in a business plan is that it provides **clarity and focus**. The business plan offers a structured format where each objective can be broken down into smaller, actionable tasks, making it easier to understand how these objectives will be achieved. Without this structure, strategic objectives may remain abstract, leading to confusion among team members about how to contribute to the company's long-term goals. By embedding these objectives into the business plan, the company can provide clear direction, ensuring that everyone understands their role in moving the business forward.

Another advantage of defining strategic objectives in the business plan is that it encourages **accountability**. A well-crafted business plan outlines specific targets, timelines, and key performance indicators (KPIs) that make it possible to track progress toward each strategic objective. This level of detail creates a culture of accountability within the organization, as managers and employees are held responsible for achieving the milestones set out in the plan. Regular reviews of the business plan allow leadership to assess whether the company is on track to meet its objectives or if adjustments need to be made. This focus on measurable outcomes ensures that strategic objectives are not just aspirational but actionable, driving tangible results.

Additionally, incorporating strategic objectives into the business plan enables **resource allocation** to be more efficient. Every business operates with limited resources, whether that be financial capital, time, or manpower. By defining strategic objectives within the business plan, the company can allocate resources in a way that aligns with its long-term goals. For example, if one of the strategic objectives is to expand into new markets, the business plan would detail the resources required for market research, product development, and marketing initiatives. This structured approach ensures that resources are not wasted on initiatives that do not contribute to the overall strategy, allowing the company to focus its efforts on the areas that will have the greatest impact.

Moreover, defining strategic objectives in a business plan makes it easier to **communicate with external stakeholders**, including investors, partners, and customers. A well-organized business plan that clearly articulates the company's strategic objectives provides confidence to investors that the business has a clear direction and a practical approach to achieving its goals. It demonstrates that the company's leadership has thought through the challenges and opportunities ahead and has a concrete plan for addressing them. This transparency not only helps attract investment but also builds trust with partners and customers, who can see that the company is serious about delivering on its promises.

In conclusion, defining strategic objectives within the context of a business plan is essential for providing clarity, accountability, resource alignment, and effective communication. It transforms high-level goals into actionable steps, ensuring that the company has a practical path to achieving its vision. A business plan serves as the foundation for turning strategic objectives into measurable, attainable outcomes that drive long-term success.

Coherence with the Company's Strategy and Vision

The success of any organization relies heavily on the **coherence between its strategic objectives, overall strategy, and long-term vision**. Coherence ensures that every action the company takes is aligned with its broader mission and helps the business move toward its ultimate goals. Without this alignment, companies can find themselves pursuing initiatives that, while potentially profitable in the short term, may not support the long-term sustainability and growth of the business. Ensuring coherence between strategy, objectives, and vision creates a unified direction for the entire organization.
Coherence begins with a clear **understanding of the company's vision**. The vision represents the future aspirations of the company—what it wants to become and the impact it hopes to have on its industry or society at large. For example, a company that envisions becoming a leader in sustainable products will shape its strategies and objectives around sustainability. The company's vision serves as a guiding star, ensuring that every strategic decision, whether related to product development, market expansion, or operational efficiency, supports this long-term goal.

Strategic objectives are the **specific, actionable steps** that help the company move closer to realizing its vision. These objectives must be coherent with the broader strategy, which outlines how the company plans to compete in its market and achieve its goals. For instance, if a company's vision is to become the top provider of eco-friendly consumer goods, its strategic objectives might include launching a new line of sustainable products, reducing the environmental impact of its supply chain, and improving energy efficiency in its manufacturing processes. These objectives directly support the overarching strategy of focusing on sustainability as a competitive advantage. One of the most significant benefits of coherence between strategy and objectives is that it allows for **efficient decision-making**. When the strategic objectives are well-aligned with the company's vision and overall strategy, leadership can make decisions more easily, knowing that their choices support the broader mission of the organization. This alignment reduces the risk of pursuing projects or initiatives that may seem promising in isolation but do not contribute to the company's long-term success. Coherence ensures that every decision made at both the tactical and strategic levels works toward the same ultimate goal, preventing wasted resources and effort on initiatives that do not align with the company's vision. Moreover, coherence helps build a **strong organizational culture**. When employees understand how their daily tasks and responsibilities contribute to the company's long-term objectives, they are more engaged and motivated. A coherent strategy fosters a sense of purpose among employees, as they can see how their work fits into the bigger picture. This alignment creates a unified team that is focused on achieving the company's vision, driving both individual and organizational performance.

Coherence between strategy and vision also enhances the company's ability to **adapt to change**. In today's rapidly evolving business environment, companies must be flexible and responsive to new opportunities and challenges. A coherent strategy ensures that even when the company needs to pivot or make adjustments, it remains aligned with its long-term vision. For example, if market conditions shift and the company needs to explore new distribution channels or product offerings, a coherent strategy will guide these changes in a way that still supports the company's overall mission. This flexibility, rooted in a strong alignment between vision and strategy, allows the company to remain resilient and focused even in times of uncertainty.

In summary, ensuring coherence between strategic objectives, company strategy, and the long-term vision is critical for sustainable success. It aligns every action the company takes with its overarching mission, enabling efficient decision-making, fostering a strong organizational culture, and allowing for adaptability in the face of change. Coherence ensures that the company stays on course to achieve its ultimate goals while navigating the complexities of a dynamic business environment.

Chapter 4: Creating Action Plans Coherent with the Strategic Vision

Creating Action Plans Coherent with the Strategic Vision

Once a company has established its strategic vision, the next critical step is to translate that vision into concrete, actionable steps. This is where **creating action plans** comes into play. Action plans are the detailed roadmaps that define how the company will achieve its strategic objectives and, ultimately, its vision. For action plans to be effective, they must be directly **coherent with the strategic vision**, ensuring that every task and initiative moves the company closer to its long-term goals.

The key to creating action plans that align with the strategic vision is **clarity and specificity**. Each action plan should break down broader strategic objectives into smaller, manageable tasks that are clearly defined and assigned to specific individuals or teams. For example, if a company's strategic vision is to become a leader in eco-friendly products, an action plan might outline specific initiatives such as developing new sustainable materials, improving supply chain transparency, or launching a marketing campaign that emphasizes the environmental benefits of the products. These tasks would be laid out step-by-step, ensuring that everyone involved knows exactly what needs to be done and how their work contributes to the overall mission.

In addition to clarity, action plans must be **time-bound**. Setting clear deadlines for each task is essential for keeping the organization on track and ensuring that progress is being made. Without a sense of urgency, even the most well-crafted plans can lose momentum, causing delays that can ultimately derail the company's ability to achieve its long-term vision. Timeframes should be realistic but challenging, motivating teams to stay focused and deliver results. Moreover, action plans should be **adaptable**. While it is crucial to have a structured plan in place, businesses operate in dynamic environments where market conditions, customer preferences, and competitive landscapes can change rapidly. Action plans must be flexible enough to allow for adjustments when necessary, ensuring that the company can pivot without losing sight of its strategic vision. For example, if a new technology emerges that could enhance product sustainability, the company should be prepared to integrate that innovation into its action plan, keeping it aligned with the broader goal of leadership in eco-friendly products.

In summary, creating action plans coherent with the strategic vision is a vital process that ensures every task contributes to the company's long-term goals. By breaking down strategic objectives into clear, time-bound tasks and remaining adaptable to change, businesses can maintain focus and momentum, moving steadily toward the realization of their vision.

What are Strategic Action Plans

Strategic action plans are detailed, step-by-step guides that outline how a company will execute its strategic objectives. They are the practical tools that translate high-level goals into actionable tasks, providing a clear path for achieving the company's long-term vision. Unlike broader strategic plans, which focus on setting goals and defining the direction of the company, strategic action plans focus on **execution**—detailing the specific actions that need to be taken, who is responsible for them, and the timeline for completion.

The primary purpose of a strategic action plan is to ensure that the company's strategic objectives are **achievable** by breaking them down into manageable, measurable tasks. Each action plan should be specific enough that there is no ambiguity about what needs to be done. For example, if the strategic objective is to increase market share in a new geographic region, the action plan might include tasks such as conducting market research, hiring local sales staff, building partnerships with regional distributors, and launching a localized marketing campaign. Each of these tasks would be assigned to a team or individual, with clear deadlines and performance metrics to track progress.

Strategic action plans also provide a framework for **resource allocation**. They help ensure that the company's resources—whether financial, human, or technological—are used efficiently to achieve the most important objectives. By outlining specific tasks and timelines, the action plan allows leadership to allocate resources where they are most needed, ensuring that there is no overlap or waste. For instance, if a key part of the action plan involves developing a new product line, resources can be focused on research and development, rather than on unrelated areas that do not contribute directly to the strategic goal.

Another critical element of strategic action plans is that they foster **accountability** within the organization. Each task within the plan is assigned to a specific individual or team, creating clear lines of responsibility. This not only ensures that everyone knows what is expected of them but also provides a mechanism for tracking progress and holding individuals accountable for delivering results. Regular progress reviews, performance metrics, and feedback loops are essential components of this process, ensuring that any potential issues are identified and addressed early, before they impact the overall success of the strategy.

In conclusion, strategic action plans are essential tools for turning high-level strategic objectives into concrete results. By providing a clear, detailed roadmap for execution, they ensure that the company's efforts are focused, efficient, and accountable. With well-crafted action plans in place, businesses can more effectively implement their strategies and move toward achieving their long-term vision.

Why You Should Set Action Plans and Responsibilities

Setting **action plans and responsibilities** is crucial for the successful execution of any business strategy. Action plans provide the blueprint for achieving the company's strategic objectives, while clearly defined responsibilities ensure that every task is completed efficiently and on time. Without a well-structured action plan and clear assignment of duties, even the best-laid strategies can fall apart due to confusion, lack of accountability, or missed deadlines.

One of the main reasons for setting action plans is that they ensure **structured progress**. By outlining specific tasks, timelines, and the individuals or teams responsible for each, action plans prevent the organization from becoming overwhelmed by the complexity of its strategic goals. Instead of trying to achieve everything at once, action plans break down the strategy into smaller, manageable pieces, allowing for a step-by-step approach. For example, if the company's objective is to launch a new product line within the next year, the action plan might divide this goal into stages—product development, market research, production, marketing, and distribution— each with its own timeline and set of responsibilities.

Clearly defined responsibilities are equally important because they ensure **accountability**. When tasks are assigned to specific individuals or teams, it becomes easier to track progress and hold people accountable for delivering results. This eliminates ambiguity and ensures that everyone understands their role in achieving the company's strategic objectives. For instance, in a marketing campaign, one team might be responsible for digital advertising, another for social media engagement, and another for public relations. By clearly defining these roles, the company can ensure that all aspects of the campaign are covered and that there is no duplication of effort or gaps in execution.

Another reason to set action plans and responsibilities is that it fosters **collaboration and coordination** within the organization. When everyone knows what tasks need to be completed and who is responsible for them, it becomes easier to coordinate efforts across different departments or teams. This is particularly important in large organizations where multiple teams may be working on different aspects of the same strategic objective. For example, the product development team needs to work closely with the marketing and sales teams to ensure that the new product launch is aligned with customer needs and market trends. Clear action plans and responsibilities facilitate communication and collaboration, ensuring that everyone is working toward the same goal.

Finally, setting action plans and responsibilities helps with **performance measurement and improvement**. By tracking the progress of each task against the timeline and objectives outlined in the action plan, leadership can quickly identify any areas where the company is falling behind or where additional resources may be needed. This allows for timely adjustments, preventing small issues from becoming major roadblocks. It also provides a basis for performance reviews and continuous improvement, as teams can analyze what worked well and what didn't, refining their approach for future initiatives.
In summary, setting action plans and responsibilities is essential for ensuring structured progress, accountability, collaboration, and performance measurement. It transforms strategic goals into concrete, actionable steps and provides a clear framework for achieving success. Without these elements, businesses risk losing focus and direction, making it much harder to reach their long-term objectives.

Creating an Organizational Chart by Function, Division, Product, or Target Market

An **organizational chart** is a visual representation of a company's structure, showing the relationships and hierarchy between different roles, departments, or teams. Creating an organizational chart is essential for ensuring that everyone within the organization understands their position, their responsibilities, and how they fit into the broader structure. Depending on the nature of the business, the organizational chart can be created based on **function, division, product, or target market**—each approach offering different advantages depending on the company's strategic goals and operational needs.

When organizing by **function**, the chart is structured around key business areas such as marketing, sales, finance, human resources, and operations. This is one of the most common organizational structures, particularly for companies that operate within a single industry or focus on a narrow range of products or services. For example, in a manufacturing company, the functional structure might include departments like production, quality control, procurement, and logistics. The main advantage of this approach is that it allows for specialization within each function, as employees in each department can focus on improving their specific area of expertise. Additionally, a function-based organizational chart often leads to better coordination and communication within departments, as team members share similar goals and skills.

Alternatively, an organizational chart can be structured by **division**, particularly in large companies with diverse product lines or services. In this case, each division operates almost like a separate business unit, with its own functional departments such as sales, marketing, and operations. For example, a multinational corporation that produces both consumer electronics and home appliances might have separate divisions for each product category. Each division would have its own leadership team, budget, and objectives, allowing for more focused management and strategy development. The divisional structure is particularly effective for companies that need to tailor their strategies to different markets or products, as it allows each division to operate independently while still being part of the larger organization.

Another approach is organizing by **product**. This is ideal for companies that offer a wide range of products or services, each with its own unique market and operational requirements. For example, a company that sells both outdoor sports equipment and apparel might create separate organizational structures for each product line, with teams dedicated to product development, marketing, and distribution for each category. This allows for more focused attention on the specific needs of each product, ensuring that the right resources and strategies are in place to maximize performance in each category.

Finally, some companies choose to structure their organization by **target market**. This is particularly useful for businesses that serve multiple customer segments with very different needs. For instance, a software company might have separate teams focused on enterprise clients, small businesses, and individual consumers. Each market segment would have its own dedicated sales, marketing, and customer service teams, allowing the company to tailor its approach to the unique preferences and buying behaviors of each group. This approach ensures that each target market receives personalized attention, which can lead to higher customer satisfaction and loyalty.

In conclusion, creating an organizational chart by function, division, product, or target market is a vital step in structuring a business for efficiency and growth. Each approach offers unique advantages depending on the company's goals, products, and customer base. By clearly defining roles, responsibilities, and reporting relationships, an organizational chart helps ensure that the company operates smoothly and that everyone is aligned with the company's strategic objectives.

Chapter 5: Writing a Description of the Business or Entrepreneurial Activity

Writing a Description of the Business or Entrepreneurial Activity

Writing a clear and comprehensive **description of the business or entrepreneurial activity** is a critical component of any business plan. This section provides an overview of what the business does, its core products or services, and the value it offers to customers. A well-written business description not only helps potential investors, partners, and stakeholders understand the business but also serves as a blueprint for the company's operations and strategic decisions.

A business description should begin by outlining the **basic nature of the business**—whether it is a product-based company, a service provider, or a combination of both. This is followed by a detailed explanation of the key offerings, including how these products or services solve specific problems or meet the needs of customers. For example, if the business is an e-commerce platform selling sustainable home goods, the description would emphasize the range of products, such as eco-friendly kitchenware, and highlight how these items align with growing consumer demand for sustainable living.

In addition to detailing the core offerings, the description should also provide context about the **market and industry** in which the business operates. This includes information about the target audience, market trends, and the competitive landscape. For instance, a business that focuses on outdoor adventure gear might highlight the increasing popularity of outdoor activities and the demand for durable, high-quality equipment among outdoor enthusiasts. Understanding the market helps frame the business within a broader context, showing how it fits into industry trends and meets customer needs. Another important aspect of the business description is explaining the **company's structure and business model**. This includes outlining the ownership structure—whether it's a sole proprietorship, partnership, or corporation—and explaining how the company generates revenue. For example, a software-as-a-service (SaaS) business might offer a subscription-based model, where customers pay a monthly fee for access to the platform. Clarifying the business model ensures that stakeholders understand how the company operates and how it plans to generate profits.

Finally, the business description should touch on the company's **mission and long-term goals**. This helps convey the vision behind the business and provides insight into its future direction. Whether the goal is to expand into new markets, develop new products, or become a leader in a specific industry, articulating these ambitions can inspire confidence among investors and partners.

In summary, writing a detailed description of the business or entrepreneurial activity is essential for conveying the essence of the company. It not only informs stakeholders about what the business does but also helps define its strategic direction, positioning it for success in its market.

Definition of Entrepreneur (According to Civil Code)

In legal terms, the definition of an **entrepreneur** varies by jurisdiction, but most civil codes around the world recognize an entrepreneur as an individual or entity engaged in economic activity for the purpose of generating profit. According to the **Civil Code**, an entrepreneur is defined as someone who organizes, manages, and assumes the risks of a business or enterprise. This definition encapsulates the core responsibilities and challenges of entrepreneurship: identifying opportunities, creating value, and taking on the financial risk of running a business.

The **Civil Code** often stipulates that an entrepreneur can be a sole proprietor, a partnership, or a corporation, depending on how the business is structured. Regardless of the legal form, the entrepreneur is the key decision-maker who determines the direction of the business. Entrepreneurs are responsible for organizing resources—capital, labor, and materials—into a productive enterprise that offers goods or services in exchange for revenue. This role involves not only operational decision-making but also strategic planning, financial management, and marketing.

Moreover, the Civil Code emphasizes that the entrepreneur assumes **economic risk**. Unlike employees, who receive a fixed salary, entrepreneurs face uncertainty about the success of their ventures. They invest their own resources, or resources obtained from investors, with the understanding that their business might fail or succeed. This risk-taking aspect is one of the defining characteristics of entrepreneurship. Entrepreneurs must navigate fluctuating market conditions, changing consumer preferences, and competitive pressures, all while seeking to turn a profit.

The **Civil Code** also recognizes the entrepreneur's role in **innovation and market competition**. Entrepreneurs often introduce new products, services, or business models that disrupt existing markets and create new value for consumers. By doing so, they contribute to economic growth, job creation, and technological advancement. In many cases, governments provide specific legal frameworks, tax benefits, or financial incentives to support entrepreneurs because of their role in driving innovation and economic development.

In conclusion, according to the Civil Code, an entrepreneur is someone who organizes and operates a business, assuming the financial risks and responsibilities that come with it. Entrepreneurs are central to economic activity, playing a critical role in innovation, competition, and the generation of wealth.

Definition of Business (According to Civil Code)

The **Civil Code** typically defines a **business** as any organized activity conducted for the purpose of producing goods or providing services in exchange for compensation. This definition underscores the structured nature of business operations and highlights the central goal of profit generation. The key elements that characterize a business include the organization of resources, the production or sale of goods and services, and the intention to make a profit.
Under the Civil Code, a business is viewed as a legal entity that can take different forms, including sole proprietorships, partnerships, limited liability companies (LLCs), or corporations. Each of these structures carries different legal implications, particularly in terms of liability, tax obligations, and governance. For instance, in a sole proprietorship, the business owner has unlimited liability, meaning that personal assets can be used to settle business debts. In contrast, a corporation is treated as a separate legal entity, where shareholders are only liable for their investment in the company, protecting their personal assets from business liabilities.

One of the defining features of a business, according to the Civil Code, is the **profit motive**. While businesses can engage in charitable or social activities, their primary purpose is typically to generate financial returns for their owners or shareholders. This means that businesses must effectively manage their resources—labor, capital, and materials—to produce goods or services efficiently and at a price that exceeds their costs. Profitability is the driving force behind most business activities, providing the incentive for innovation, expansion, and competition.

Another important aspect recognized by the Civil Code is the **systematic organization** of business activities. This means that businesses must operate in a structured and regular manner, with processes in place for production, distribution, marketing, and management. Whether a business is producing tangible goods like electronics or intangible services like consulting, the operations must be organized and consistent to ensure sustainability and growth. This organizational aspect differentiates businesses from informal economic activities, which may not be structured or ongoing.

The Civil Code also addresses the **legal obligations** of businesses, such as tax requirements, labor laws, and consumer protections. Businesses must comply with these regulations to operate legally and maintain their standing in the marketplace. These legal frameworks are designed to protect not only the business itself but also its customers, employees, and the broader economy.

In summary, according to the Civil Code, a business is an organized activity aimed at producing goods or services for profit. It operates within a legal framework that defines its structure, responsibilities, and rights, ensuring that it functions in a manner that benefits both the owners and the economy as a whole.

Through the Practice of Writing, Stimulating a Virtuous Cycle for Business Plan Development

The act of **writing a business plan** is not merely a formality; it serves as a powerful tool for stimulating what can be described as a **virtuous cycle** of development and refinement. The process of writing forces entrepreneurs and business leaders to think critically about their goals, strategies, and operations, leading to clearer decision-making and more effective execution. As the business grows and evolves, the business plan serves as both a reference point and a roadmap, guiding ongoing adjustments and improvements.

Writing encourages **clarity and precision**. When drafting a business plan, entrepreneurs must articulate their vision, mission, objectives, and strategies in a coherent and structured manner. This forces them to refine their ideas, removing any vagueness or ambiguity that might otherwise hinder the business's development. For example, writing a detailed section on market analysis requires the entrepreneur to thoroughly research their target audience, understand competitors, and assess industry trends. This level of detail sharpens the entrepreneur's understanding of their environment, leading to more informed decisions about how to position the business for success.

Moreover, the practice of writing stimulates **self-reflection and analysis**. As entrepreneurs outline their business's strengths, weaknesses, opportunities, and threats (SWOT analysis), they are prompted to assess the current state of the business objectively. This reflective process helps identify potential risks and challenges that might not have been apparent before. By confronting these issues during the planning stage, entrepreneurs can devise strategies to mitigate risks and capitalize on opportunities. For instance, a business might recognize a gap in its marketing strategy or an emerging trend in consumer behavior that it can exploit to gain a competitive advantage.

The cyclical nature of business plan development also fosters **continuous improvement**. A business plan is not a static document; it should be revisited and updated regularly as the business evolves and market conditions change. Each time the plan is revised, new insights are gained, and previous strategies are re-evaluated. This continuous cycle of writing, reviewing, and revising keeps the business plan relevant and ensures that the company remains agile and responsive to changes in the marketplace. For example, if a new competitor enters the market, the business can adjust its strategies to protect its market share or differentiate itself more effectively.

Furthermore, writing a business plan creates a **sense of accountability**. When objectives and action plans are written down, it becomes easier to track progress and measure success. This encourages entrepreneurs to stay focused on their goals and motivates them to follow through on their commitments. In a team setting, a written plan ensures that everyone understands their roles and responsibilities, promoting better collaboration and coordination.

In conclusion, writing a business plan stimulates a virtuous cycle of clarity, reflection, and continuous improvement. By forcing entrepreneurs to articulate their ideas clearly and systematically, the process of writing helps refine strategies, identify challenges, and ensure that the business remains adaptable and focused on long-term success.

Clarity of Business Ideas and Plans

Achieving **clarity of business ideas and plans** is essential for the success of any entrepreneurial venture. A clear business idea not only defines what the business aims to accomplish but also provides a solid foundation for all subsequent planning and execution. Without clarity, businesses risk losing direction, confusing stakeholders, and missing opportunities for growth. On the other hand, a well-defined business idea guides every aspect of the business, from strategy to operations, and ensures that the company remains focused on its goals. Clarity in business ideas begins with a detailed understanding of the **problem or need** the business seeks to address. Successful businesses typically emerge from a clear identification of a market gap or a customer pain point. For example, an entrepreneur might notice that there is a growing demand for eco-friendly home products but that current options are either too expensive or not readily available. A clear business idea would aim to solve this problem by offering affordable, accessible, and high-quality sustainable home goods. The more precise the business idea, the easier it becomes to communicate its value to customers, investors, and partners.

Once the business idea is clearly defined, the next step is to create a **business plan** that outlines how the idea will be turned into a viable enterprise. The business plan should cover several critical components, including the target market, value proposition, revenue model, and marketing strategy. For instance, if the business idea involves providing a subscription service for eco-friendly products, the business plan would detail how the service will operate, the pricing structure, how customers will be acquired, and how the business will generate profits over time. The plan should provide clarity on the business's **short-term objectives** as well as its **long-term vision**.

Clarity also means ensuring that all aspects of the business plan are **coherent and aligned**. Each section of the plan should support the others. For example, the marketing strategy should align with the target market identified in the business model, and the financial projections should be realistic based on the pricing strategy and expected customer acquisition rates. Any inconsistencies or vague areas within the business plan can create confusion, making it harder to secure funding, hire talent, or grow the business effectively.

Another critical aspect of clarity is **communication**. A clear business idea and plan make it easier to communicate with various stakeholders, from potential investors to team members. Investors, in particular, are more likely to support a business that can articulate its goals, strategies, and potential for growth in a concise and compelling way. Employees also benefit from clarity, as they understand the company's direction and their role within it, leading to better engagement and performance.

In conclusion, clarity in business ideas and plans is vital for laying a strong foundation for growth and success. By ensuring that the business idea is well-defined and that the plan is coherent and actionable, entrepreneurs can create a roadmap that guides their efforts, attracts investment, and ensures that everyone involved in the business is aligned toward achieving its goals.

Definition of Activities

In any business, the **definition of activities** plays a crucial role in ensuring that operations are efficient, organized, and aligned with the company's overall strategy. Defining activities involves clearly identifying the tasks and processes that need to be performed to achieve the business's objectives. Whether it's product development, marketing, sales, customer service, or financial management, each activity should be mapped out in detail to ensure that resources are allocated effectively and that everyone understands their role in the organization.

The first step in defining business activities is to break down the company's operations into **functional areas**. For example, a retail business might have distinct activities related to procurement, inventory management, sales, and customer service. Each of these functional areas represents a set of tasks that contribute to the smooth running of the business. By clearly defining what each area is responsible for, businesses can ensure that there are no overlaps or gaps in operations. This also helps in creating specialized teams or departments that focus on specific aspects of the business, improving overall efficiency and productivity.

Next, it's important to establish the **objectives and outputs** of each activity. For example, the marketing department's activities might include creating promotional campaigns, managing social media accounts, and conducting market research. The objective of these activities would be to increase brand awareness, attract new customers, and ultimately drive sales. Clearly defining the expected outcomes of each activity helps ensure that everyone involved understands what they are working toward and how their efforts contribute to the business's success.

Another essential aspect of defining activities is identifying the **tools, resources, and processes** required to carry them out. For instance, if one of the key activities in the business is product development, the company must ensure that it has access to the right materials, technology, and expertise to design and manufacture products efficiently. Similarly, sales activities might require customer relationship management (CRM) software, a well-trained sales team, and a strategy for engaging potential clients. By detailing the necessary resources, businesses can ensure that each activity is adequately supported and can be carried out without unnecessary delays or obstacles.

In addition to defining core activities, it's also important to establish how these activities are **monitored and evaluated**. This typically involves setting key performance indicators (KPIs) for each function. For example, a KPI for customer service might be the average response time to customer inquiries, while a KPI for production could be the number of units produced per day. Monitoring these indicators allows the business to track its performance and make adjustments as needed to improve efficiency and achieve its objectives.

In conclusion, the definition of activities is a fundamental part of business operations. By clearly identifying tasks, objectives, resources, and performance metrics, businesses can ensure that their activities are aligned with their strategic goals, improving efficiency and driving growth.

"Who Does What" Approach to Include in the Company Description

The **"Who Does What"** approach is an essential element of any **company description**, as it clarifies the roles and responsibilities within the organization. By outlining exactly who is responsible for each function and task, this approach helps create structure, accountability, and clarity across all levels of the business. For both internal team members and external stakeholders, understanding who is in charge of what ensures that the company operates efficiently, with minimal confusion about duties or decision-making processes.

Incorporating the "Who Does What" approach into the company description starts with identifying the **key roles and positions** within the organization. This can be based on the company's functional areas, such as marketing, sales, finance, operations, and human resources. Each function should have a clearly defined leader or team responsible for its execution. For example, a company might assign a Chief Marketing Officer (CMO) to oversee all marketing activities, while the Chief Financial Officer (CFO) manages financial planning and reporting. By clearly identifying these roles in the company description, the business ensures that every aspect of its operations has a designated leader who is accountable for its performance.

Next, the "Who Does What" approach requires detailing the **specific responsibilities** associated with each role. For instance, within the marketing department, the CMO might be responsible for developing the overall marketing strategy, while a social media manager would handle the day-to-day management of social media channels, and a content strategist would focus on creating marketing materials such as blogs, videos, and advertisements. By breaking down responsibilities to this level of detail, the company ensures that tasks are properly delegated and that everyone understands their specific duties. This also helps avoid overlaps or confusion about who is responsible for which tasks, reducing inefficiencies and improving overall productivity.

In addition to internal clarity, the "Who Does What" approach is particularly useful when presenting the company to **external stakeholders** such as investors, partners, or customers. Investors, for example, want to see that the company has a well-structured team in place with clear roles and responsibilities. They are more likely to invest in a business that demonstrates strong leadership and effective delegation of tasks. Likewise, customers and partners benefit from knowing who to contact for specific needs or inquiries. If a customer has a question about a product, knowing who is responsible for customer service or sales can streamline communication and improve the overall customer experience.

Another advantage of the "Who Does What" approach is that it helps establish a **clear chain of command**. In any business, there will be times when decisions need to be made quickly, and having a well-defined organizational structure ensures that decisions can be made efficiently without unnecessary delays. For instance, if a critical decision needs to be made about product development, it should be clear whether the final decision rests with the Chief Product Officer or another executive. This level of clarity helps prevent bottlenecks and ensures that the company can respond quickly to challenges or opportunities.

In conclusion, the "Who Does What" approach is a vital part of the company description that ensures clarity, accountability, and efficiency. By clearly defining roles and responsibilities, businesses can operate more smoothly, improve communication both internally and externally, and create a structured environment where decision-making is streamlined and responsibilities are well understood.

Chapter 6: Conducting a Market Analysis Using Appropriate Tools

Market analysis is a crucial step in developing a successful business strategy. It involves researching and evaluating the external environment in which the business operates to identify opportunities, threats, and competitive forces. By understanding the market, businesses can make informed decisions about positioning, product development, pricing, and expansion. Several analytical tools are widely used in market analysis, including the **SWOT Analysis**, **Porter's Five Forces Model**, and the **Boston Consulting Group (BCG) Matrix**. Each of these tools provides unique insights into different aspects of the market and can help guide strategic planning.

A thorough market analysis helps businesses:
- Identify trends and patterns in customer behavior.
- Understand the competitive landscape.
- Assess potential risks and opportunities.
- Determine the most effective strategies for growth and sustainability.

By using the right tools, businesses can break down complex market dynamics into actionable insights, improving their chances of success in a competitive environment.

SWOT Analysis

The **SWOT Analysis** is one of the most widely used tools for market analysis. SWOT stands for **Strengths, Weaknesses, Opportunities, and Threats**, and it provides a framework for assessing both the internal and external factors that affect a business. This analysis helps businesses understand where they excel, where they need improvement, and how they can leverage opportunities while mitigating risks.

- **Strengths** refer to the internal factors that give the company a competitive edge. These could include a strong brand reputation, a loyal customer base, proprietary technology, or skilled employees. Identifying strengths helps businesses capitalize on what they do best. For example, a company with a reputation for high-quality customer service can use that strength to differentiate itself from competitors.
- **Weaknesses** are internal factors that may hinder the business's success. These might include limited financial resources, outdated technology, or poor market penetration. Recognizing weaknesses allows companies to address them proactively. For instance, if a business identifies weak marketing as a vulnerability, it can allocate more resources toward developing a stronger marketing strategy.
- **Opportunities** represent external factors that the company can exploit to achieve growth. These could be emerging market trends, changes in customer preferences, or new technologies. By identifying opportunities, businesses can position themselves to take advantage of favorable conditions. For example, a growing demand for eco-friendly products presents an opportunity for

companies in the sustainability sector to introduce innovative green solutions.
- **Threats** are external factors that pose risks to the business. These might include new competitors, economic downturns, or regulatory changes. Identifying threats allows businesses to prepare contingency plans and reduce the potential impact. For example, a company facing increased competition might invest in research and development to innovate and stay ahead in the market.

A **SWOT analysis** is particularly valuable because it provides a balanced view of both internal and external factors. It encourages businesses to take a comprehensive look at their position in the market, helping them build on their strengths, shore up their weaknesses, capitalize on opportunities, and defend against threats. This tool is flexible and can be used for various aspects of the business, from launching new products to entering new markets.

Porter's Model Analysis

Porter's Five Forces Model, developed by Michael Porter, is a powerful tool for analyzing the **competitive forces** in an industry. It helps businesses understand the intensity of competition and the potential profitability of entering or expanding within a market. The model identifies five key forces that shape the competitive landscape:

1. **Threat of New Entrants**: This force examines how easily new competitors can enter the market. If entry barriers are low, such as minimal capital requirements or lenient regulations, the threat of new entrants is high, increasing competition. Businesses need to consider how they can create barriers to entry, such as strong branding, customer loyalty, or proprietary technology, to protect their market position.

2. **Bargaining Power of Suppliers**: This force assesses how much power suppliers have over a business. If there are few suppliers of critical inputs or if switching suppliers is difficult, suppliers can exert significant influence, potentially raising costs. Companies with multiple sourcing options or the ability to negotiate favorable terms are in a stronger position. For example, businesses that rely on specialized components may face higher supplier power, whereas those with access to many vendors can minimize this risk.

3. **Bargaining Power of Buyers**: This force looks at how much influence customers have over pricing and product quality. When buyers are concentrated or have many alternative options, their bargaining power increases. For instance, in highly competitive markets, such as consumer electronics, customers

can demand better prices and higher quality, forcing businesses to adapt.
4. **Threat of Substitute Products or Services**: This force evaluates the likelihood of customers switching to alternative products or services. When substitutes are readily available and offer a similar value proposition, businesses face a higher risk of losing market share. Companies must innovate and differentiate their products to mitigate this threat. For example, a soda company might face a threat from healthier beverage options, such as bottled water or natural juices.
5. **Industry Rivalry**: This force considers the intensity of competition among existing players. Highly competitive industries with many competitors often engage in price wars, marketing battles, and product innovation races.
Understanding the level of industry rivalry helps businesses develop strategies to stand out. For example, in the airline industry, intense rivalry forces companies to offer competitive pricing, customer service enhancements, and loyalty programs.

By analyzing these five forces, businesses can gain a deeper understanding of the competitive dynamics in their industry and develop strategies to improve their market position. Porter's model is especially useful for businesses looking to enter a new market or assess the risks and rewards of their current competitive environment.

Boston Consulting Group Matrix Analysis

The **Boston Consulting Group (BCG) Matrix** is a tool used to assess a company's product portfolio and determine the best allocation of resources. It categorizes products or business units into four quadrants based on **market growth rate** and **market share**. This analysis helps businesses decide which products to invest in, which to maintain, and which to phase out.

1. **Stars**: Products in this category have high market share and are in high-growth markets. Stars are often the focus of a company's investment because they have the potential to generate significant revenue in the future. However, they also require substantial investment to maintain their growth. For example, a technology company might classify its newest, rapidly growing software product as a Star, warranting further investment in development and marketing.
2. **Cash Cows**: These products have high market share but are in low-growth markets. Cash Cows generate steady, reliable cash flow with minimal investment. The strategy here is to "milk" these products for profits to fund other areas of the business. For example, a well-established consumer goods company may have mature product lines, such as toothpaste or detergent, that provide consistent profits.
3. **Question Marks**: These products are in high-growth markets but have low market share. They have potential but require significant investment to increase market share. Businesses must decide whether to invest in Question Marks to turn them into Stars or divest if the prospects are not promising. For instance, a startup with a new,

unproven product might categorize it as a Question Mark while deciding whether to allocate more resources to its development.
4. **Dogs**: Products in this quadrant have low market share and operate in low-growth markets. These products are often considered for divestment or discontinuation because they consume resources without delivering significant returns. For example, a company might phase out an outdated product that no longer meets customer needs or competes effectively in the market.

The BCG Matrix helps businesses allocate resources more effectively by focusing on products with the highest potential for growth and profitability. It encourages strategic decision-making by highlighting which products deserve further investment and which ones should be scaled back or eliminated.

In conclusion, conducting a market analysis using tools like **SWOT Analysis**, **Porter's Five Forces**, and the **BCG Matrix** provides businesses with critical insights into their market environment and competitive position. Each tool serves a different purpose but together they offer a comprehensive approach to understanding internal strengths and weaknesses, external opportunities and threats, competitive pressures, and the strategic allocation of resources. By leveraging these tools, businesses can make more informed decisions and develop strategies that align with their long-term goals.

Chapter 7: Listing Your Products & Services

A critical aspect of building a successful business is the clear and strategic **listing of your products and services**. This involves taking your core business idea and transforming it into specific offerings that address customer needs and market demands. Defining and listing products and services goes beyond simply cataloging what you sell; it's about aligning your offerings with market trends, customer preferences, and the broader business strategy.

The product and service listings should reflect the unique value your business provides, helping potential customers understand how your offerings can meet their needs better than the competition. Whether you are launching a new product, repositioning an existing one, or expanding into new markets, having a clear, well-structured product and service list is essential for marketing, sales, and overall business growth.

From the Business Idea to Writing the Key Products to Launch or Reposition in the Market(s)

Taking a **business idea** from concept to market requires careful planning and execution, particularly when it comes to **writing the key products to launch or reposition**. This process begins by identifying how your initial business idea translates into tangible offerings that can effectively meet the needs of your target market.

The first step is to **evaluate your business idea** through the lens of customer demand and market trends. For example, if your business idea is centered around eco-friendly consumer goods, you would need to identify specific products—such as biodegradable cleaning supplies or sustainable packaging materials—that align with both your vision and market demand. The key is to ensure that your products solve a problem or fill a gap in the market, providing value to customers.

Once the product ideas are identified, the next step is to **prioritize which products to launch first**. This decision should be guided by factors such as market readiness, production capacity, and customer interest. For instance, if the market for sustainable packaging is rapidly growing, launching your most innovative packaging product first may help you capture early market share. Alternatively, if customer research indicates strong demand for biodegradable cleaning supplies, focusing on this product line could be more advantageous.

For businesses that already have products in the market, **repositioning** can be a strategic move to adapt to changing market conditions or customer preferences. Repositioning involves altering the way a product is perceived by customers, either by highlighting new features, changing its price point, or targeting a different market segment. For example, a company that sells traditional cleaning products may reposition its offerings by reformulating them with eco-friendly ingredients and marketing them as environmentally conscious solutions.

To effectively list your products, each offering should be accompanied by a **clear product description** that highlights its features, benefits, and how it addresses customer needs. These descriptions are vital for marketing and sales purposes, as they provide potential customers with the information they need to make informed purchasing decisions. Each product listing should include:

- **Product name**: A clear and compelling name that reflects the product's core attributes.
- **Key features**: The most important aspects of the product that differentiate it from competitors.
- **Customer benefits**: How the product solves a specific problem or meets a need for the customer.
- **Target market**: A description of the ideal customer for this product.
- **Price point**: The pricing strategy for the product and its perceived value in the market.

By clearly defining your products and aligning them with market demand, you increase the likelihood of a successful launch or repositioning, setting the foundation for strong customer engagement and sales growth.

From Defining the Strategy to Writing the Key Services to Launch or Remodel in the Market(s)

In addition to products, businesses often offer **services** that complement their core offerings and provide additional value to customers. Defining your service strategy is critical to ensuring that your business remains competitive and can adapt to the evolving needs of the market. Writing the key services to launch or remodel in the market is about carefully aligning these services with both your business strategy and customer expectations.

The process starts by defining how your **business strategy** influences the types of services you offer. For example, if your business strategy emphasizes customer experience and long-term relationships, the services you offer should reflect this focus. This could include personalized customer support, after-sales service, or tailored solutions that enhance customer satisfaction and loyalty. The goal is to ensure that your services align with the overall strategic vision of your company, whether that vision involves innovation, customer service excellence, or cost leadership.

When deciding on the key services to launch, it's important to consider the **current needs of your target market**. Customer expectations are constantly evolving, and the services that were relevant last year may need to be updated or replaced. For example, in the technology sector, customers increasingly expect quick, efficient technical support and seamless onboarding processes. A company that provides software solutions might launch new services like 24/7 technical support or a comprehensive onboarding package that helps new clients integrate the software into their systems quickly and effectively.

In cases where a service already exists but needs updating, businesses can **remodel services** to better align with customer demands or improve efficiency. Remodeling services involves reevaluating how the service is delivered, whether it is meeting customer expectations, and whether it can be improved through new technology or processes. For example, a company that offers consulting services might remodel its offerings by incorporating new digital tools for remote consultations, making the service more accessible to a wider audience.

Each service should be clearly defined and **differentiated** from competitors. A well-crafted service listing includes:

- **Service name**: A concise name that accurately represents what the service offers.
- **Service description**: A detailed explanation of what the service includes and how it benefits the customer.
- **Customer benefits**: Specific ways in which the service solves a problem or adds value for the customer.
- **Delivery method**: How the service is provided—whether in-person, remotely, or through a combination of both.

- **Target audience**: The specific customer segment the service is designed for.
- **Pricing**: The cost of the service and any tiered options available, if applicable.

Writing key services to launch or remodel is also about ensuring that your offerings are **scalable** and adaptable. Services should be designed to grow with your business and meet the evolving demands of the market. For instance, if your business is entering a new geographic region, consider how your services can be customized to fit the cultural and regulatory landscape of that area.

In conclusion, whether you are launching new services or remodeling existing ones, it is essential to define how they align with your business strategy and meet the needs of your target market. By providing clear descriptions and emphasizing the unique value your services offer, you can enhance customer satisfaction and position your business for sustained growth in competitive markets.

Chapter 8: Defining a Marketing Plan

A **marketing plan** is an essential part of any business strategy. It outlines how a company intends to promote its products or services, attract customers, and achieve sales goals. A well-crafted marketing plan not only defines the actions needed to reach the target audience but also aligns with the company's overall business objectives. It involves detailed research, strategic thinking, and resource allocation to ensure that marketing efforts are both effective and efficient.

Creating a marketing plan starts by understanding the **target market**—the group of customers most likely to purchase the company's products or services. This requires an in-depth analysis of customer demographics, preferences, and behaviors. The next step is to outline the **marketing objectives**, which should align with the business's broader goals, such as increasing market share, entering new markets, or launching a new product. These objectives need to be specific, measurable, achievable, relevant, and time-bound (SMART) to guide the marketing strategy effectively.

A comprehensive marketing plan typically includes several key components:

- **Market research**: Understanding the market trends, competition, and customer needs.
- **Positioning**: Defining how the product or service stands out from competitors.
- **Budgeting**: Allocating resources for different marketing channels.
- **Metrics**: Establishing key performance indicators (KPIs) to measure success.

Ultimately, a strong marketing plan ensures that the company communicates its value proposition to the right audience, at the right time, using the most effective channels.

Conducting a Marketing Mix Analysis

A crucial element of a marketing plan is the **marketing mix analysis**, which helps businesses assess and adjust the components of their marketing strategy to meet customer needs and maximize profitability. The marketing mix typically includes four elements, often referred to as the **4Ps**: Product, Price, Promotion, and Product Distribution (Place). Together, these components form the foundation of any effective marketing strategy.

- **Product**: This refers to the actual goods or services the business offers. A successful marketing plan begins by clearly defining the product's features, benefits, and how it meets customer needs. It's also important to consider the product life cycle—whether the product is in the introduction, growth, maturity, or decline phase—because the marketing strategy will vary depending on where the product stands in its life cycle. For instance, during the introduction phase, the focus might be on raising awareness, while in the maturity phase, it might shift to differentiating the product from competitors.

- **Price**: Pricing strategy is critical in determining how a product will be perceived in the market. The price must reflect the product's value to customers while ensuring the company remains competitive and profitable. Businesses need to decide whether to pursue a **cost-based pricing strategy** (pricing based on production costs) or a **value-based pricing strategy** (pricing based on perceived customer value). Additionally, factors like market demand, competition, and customer price sensitivity should influence pricing decisions.
- **Promotion**: Promotion encompasses all the ways a business communicates with its customers to generate interest in its products or services. This includes advertising, public relations, social media marketing, sales promotions, and personal selling. A key part of the marketing mix is identifying the best promotional channels for reaching the target audience. For example, if the business targets young, tech-savvy consumers, a strong emphasis on social media marketing may be appropriate. Effective promotion ensures that potential customers are aware of the product, understand its benefits, and are motivated to make a purchase.
- **Product Distribution (Place)**: This element focuses on how the product is delivered to the customer, whether through physical stores, online platforms, or a combination of both. It's essential to ensure that the product is accessible to the target audience in the most convenient and cost-effective way. For example, an e-commerce company might focus on optimizing its website for seamless purchasing, while a brick-and-mortar business would need to ensure its products are available in locations frequented by its target customers.

By conducting a thorough marketing mix analysis, businesses can ensure that each element of their strategy is aligned with customer needs and market conditions. Adjusting any of the 4Ps based on market feedback and performance metrics is a continuous process, helping companies remain competitive and responsive to changes in consumer behavior and industry trends.

4Ps Analysis: Product, Price, Promotion, and Product Distribution

The **4Ps Analysis**—Product, Price, Promotion, and Product Distribution—serves as a framework for developing a comprehensive marketing strategy. Each "P" plays a crucial role in positioning the product or service in the market and driving customer engagement.

1. **Product**: At the core of the marketing strategy is the product itself. This involves understanding the product's features, quality, and the problem it solves for customers. It's important to assess how the product meets customer expectations and how it differentiates from competitors. In addition, businesses should regularly evaluate where the product is in its **life cycle**. New products in the introduction phase require different marketing strategies (e.g., awareness campaigns) than mature products in the saturation phase (e.g., differentiation or pricing strategies).

2. **Price**: Pricing is a critical factor in determining customer perception and market competitiveness. The pricing strategy should reflect both the value the product offers and the target market's willingness to pay. There are several approaches to pricing, including **premium pricing** (charging higher prices for high-quality or exclusive products), **penetration pricing** (setting a low price to quickly gain market share), or **skimming** (initially setting high prices and lowering them over time as competition increases). A well-structured pricing strategy can influence both market positioning and profitability.
3. **Promotion**: Promotion refers to the tactics businesses use to communicate their product's value to potential customers. This can include advertising (e.g., TV, radio, online ads), public relations (e.g., press releases, event sponsorships), and direct marketing (e.g., email campaigns, social media outreach). Effective promotion should not only create awareness but also build brand loyalty and encourage customer action, such as making a purchase or recommending the product to others. The promotion strategy should be closely aligned with the target audience's preferences and behaviors, ensuring that the business reaches its customers in the most efficient and impactful way.

4. **Product Distribution (Place)**: Product distribution focuses on how and where customers can access the product. The goal is to ensure that the product is available in the right locations, whether through retail stores, e-commerce platforms, or wholesale channels. The distribution strategy should reflect customer buying habits. For example, businesses targeting younger, tech-savvy consumers may prioritize online distribution through their own website or platforms like Amazon, while businesses catering to an older demographic may rely more on physical stores or direct sales.

By evaluating each element of the 4Ps, businesses can develop a marketing plan that aligns with their target audience and ensures that their product is positioned for success in the marketplace.

Boston Consulting Group Matrix Analysis on Product/Service Life Cycle Stages and Target Market(s)

The **Boston Consulting Group (BCG) Matrix** is a valuable tool for evaluating a company's product portfolio based on **market growth** and **market share**. It helps businesses decide where to allocate resources by classifying products or services into four categories: **Stars**, **Cash Cows**, **Question Marks**, and **Dogs**. Understanding where each product or service fits within these categories allows businesses to make informed decisions about marketing, investment, and product development.

1. **Stars**: These are products with a high market share in rapidly growing markets. Stars require significant investment to maintain their competitive advantage and to keep up with increasing demand. While they have the potential to become Cash Cows, they also consume a lot of resources. A business should focus on promoting and expanding its Stars through aggressive marketing and innovation strategies to maximize their potential. For instance, a tech company might classify its newest, most innovative software as a Star, given its potential for rapid growth and high profitability.
2. **Cash Cows**: These are products with a high market share in low-growth markets. Cash Cows generate consistent profits and require minimal investment to maintain. The goal with Cash Cows is to "milk" them for steady revenue to fund other areas of the business. Marketing efforts for Cash Cows are typically focused on maintaining customer loyalty and reinforcing the product's market position, rather than seeking significant growth.

3. **Question Marks**: These products exist in high-growth markets but have low market share. They are risky investments because they require significant resources to grow, but there's no guarantee they will succeed. Businesses must decide whether to invest in Question Marks to turn them into Stars or to divest and minimize losses. For example, a company introducing a new product in a competitive market might label it a Question Mark until it gains enough traction to become a Star or prove its viability.
4. **Dogs**: These products have low market share in low-growth markets. Dogs generate little revenue and are often considered for divestment or discontinuation. The marketing strategy for Dogs typically involves minimizing investment and redirecting resources to more promising areas of the business. Companies should carefully evaluate whether keeping a Dog in the portfolio is worth the cost, or if it's better to phase it out.

By using the BCG Matrix, businesses can effectively manage their product portfolios, ensuring that resources are allocated to products with the highest growth potential and profitability. This tool is particularly useful for businesses with multiple products or services, as it provides a clear framework for making strategic decisions based on market dynamics and the product life cycle.

In conclusion, defining a marketing plan requires a comprehensive analysis of the **4Ps**—Product, Price, Promotion, and Product Distribution—along with strategic portfolio management using tools like the **BCG Matrix**. These tools help businesses craft targeted, effective marketing strategies that align with their goals, maximize profitability, and position their products and services for success in competitive markets.

Chapter 9: Conducting Customer Segmentation

Customer segmentation is a crucial process in marketing strategy that involves dividing a broader target market into smaller, more manageable groups of customers who share similar characteristics or needs. By segmenting customers, businesses can tailor their marketing efforts, products, and services to specific groups, improving the efficiency of their campaigns and increasing customer satisfaction. Effective customer segmentation allows businesses to understand their customers better, prioritize resources, and deliver more personalized experiences. Segmentation can be based on various factors, including product or service usage, customer demographics, behavior, and geographic location. By understanding the distinct needs and preferences of each segment, companies can develop targeted strategies that resonate with specific groups, ultimately leading to higher customer loyalty and increased sales.

By Product

Segmenting customers by product is one of the most common and effective approaches, especially for businesses offering a range of products. This type of segmentation focuses on identifying which customer groups are most interested in or suited for particular products. It enables businesses to tailor marketing campaigns, product features, and sales efforts to the specific preferences and buying behaviors of different customer segments.

For example, a company that sells a variety of sports equipment might segment its customers based on the type of sport they engage in, such as running, cycling, or tennis. Each product category attracts different types of customers with unique needs. Runners may be looking for lightweight shoes with superior cushioning, while cyclists might prioritize aerodynamics and durability in their gear. By segmenting customers based on their product preferences, the company can create specialized marketing messages, promote relevant features, and design product bundles that appeal directly to these groups.

In addition to product types, businesses can also segment customers based on **product lifecycle stages**. For instance, some customers may prefer newly launched products with cutting-edge features, while others might look for well-established, reliable products. Early adopters of technology products, for example, often want the latest gadgets, while price-sensitive customers might wait for products to move through the introductory stage before making a purchase at a lower price.

Product segmentation can also be useful for identifying **upselling and cross-selling opportunities**. For example, a customer who purchases a high-end camera may also be interested in related accessories such as lenses, tripods, or carrying cases. By understanding how different products relate to one another, businesses can create targeted promotions and recommendations that encourage additional purchases, increasing the overall value of each customer.

Overall, segmenting customers by product allows businesses to focus their marketing and sales efforts on the specific needs of each product category, resulting in more relevant offers, higher customer engagement, and improved sales performance.

By Service

Service-based customer segmentation is another critical approach, particularly for businesses that provide a range of services. Just like product segmentation, this method involves identifying which customers are most likely to benefit from specific services and tailoring marketing efforts to attract and retain those customers. Service segmentation is especially useful for companies in industries such as consulting, healthcare, financial services, and technology, where different customer groups may require varying levels of service or expertise.

For instance, a consulting firm may offer services to both small businesses and large corporations, each with distinct needs. Small businesses may require basic, cost-effective consulting solutions to improve operations or marketing, while large corporations might seek more complex, customized services, such as business transformation or leadership development. By segmenting customers based on the type of service they need, the consulting firm can better allocate resources, personalize its service offerings, and market more effectively to each group.

Service segmentation is also relevant in industries like **software-as-a-service (SaaS)**, where customers can choose from different service tiers. A SaaS provider might offer basic, premium, and enterprise-level services, each designed for different customer segments. Basic users might be small businesses or individuals who need limited functionality, while enterprise customers require more robust features, dedicated support, and customization options. Segmenting customers by service tier allows the business to focus its marketing, onboarding, and customer support efforts based on the specific needs of each segment.

Moreover, businesses can segment customers based on their **service usage patterns**. For example, some customers may require frequent, hands-on support, while others might prefer self-service options. By understanding these differences, companies can adjust their service delivery models to provide the right level of engagement for each customer group, improving satisfaction and retention.

In summary, segmenting customers by service helps businesses design and deliver more personalized, relevant service experiences. By understanding the unique needs of each customer segment, companies can allocate resources effectively, improve customer satisfaction, and build stronger relationships with their clients.

By Customer Type

Segmenting customers by type is a highly effective approach that focuses on differentiating between customer groups based on characteristics such as demographics, behavior, and buying patterns. This method helps businesses understand the unique needs of each customer type and create targeted marketing strategies to engage with them more effectively. Some common customer types include individuals, businesses, government entities, or educational institutions, each with distinct purchasing behaviors and decision-making processes.

For instance, a company that sells educational technology products may segment its customers into **students**, **teachers**, and **schools**. Each of these customer types has different needs and motivations. Students might be looking for affordable, easy-to-use devices, while teachers are interested in tools that enhance learning outcomes in the classroom. Schools, on the other hand, may focus on bulk purchasing, durability, and ease of integration with existing infrastructure. By tailoring its messaging and product features to each customer type, the company can ensure that its offerings meet the specific needs of each group.

Segmentation by customer type is also valuable in **business-to-business (B2B)** markets. For example, a software company might sell its product to both small startups and large enterprises. Startups may require flexible pricing plans and scalable solutions, while large enterprises often demand more complex features, high security, and dedicated customer support. By understanding the different needs of these customer types, the software company can customize its marketing, product development, and support strategies accordingly.

Behavioral segmentation is another way to approach customer type segmentation. This method groups customers based on their behavior, such as purchasing frequency, loyalty, or spending patterns. For example, some customers might be **loyal, repeat buyers**, while others are **occasional shoppers**. Understanding these behaviors allows businesses to design personalized loyalty programs or promotions that cater to the specific habits of each customer type.

In conclusion, segmenting customers by type enables businesses to tailor their products, services, and marketing strategies to the specific needs of different customer groups. This leads to more effective engagement, better customer satisfaction, and higher conversion rates.

By Geographic Distribution

Geographic segmentation involves dividing customers based on their **location**, such as country, region, city, or even neighborhood. This type of segmentation is particularly important for businesses that operate across multiple regions or target customers with location-specific needs or preferences. Geographic segmentation helps companies understand how customer preferences and behaviors vary by location, enabling them to customize their offerings and marketing strategies to better meet local demand. For example, a company selling winter sports equipment would focus its marketing efforts in regions with cold climates and high snowfall, such as northern Europe or North America, rather than in tropical areas where the demand for such products would be minimal. Similarly, a food and beverage company might offer different product flavors or packaging sizes depending on regional preferences and consumption habits. In one region, smaller, single-serving sizes might be more popular, while in another, larger family-sized packages could be in higher demand. Geographic segmentation is also crucial for businesses that aim to **expand into new markets**. Before entering a new geographic area, companies must assess the local market conditions, including consumer preferences, competition, and economic factors. This analysis helps businesses determine whether their product or service will succeed in the new market and how to adjust their marketing strategies to fit local tastes and customs.

For companies with physical locations, geographic segmentation is key to optimizing **product distribution**. Retailers, for instance, need to ensure that their products are available in the right stores, in the right quantities, and at the right times. Understanding geographic trends allows businesses to manage their inventory more effectively, reducing waste and ensuring that high-demand areas are well-stocked.

Additionally, geographic segmentation can inform **digital marketing strategies**. Online businesses can use location-based data to tailor their digital ads, ensuring that customers in specific regions see promotions or product recommendations relevant to their location. For example, an online retailer might offer free shipping to customers in certain regions or create geo-targeted ads that highlight products that are popular in those areas.

In conclusion, geographic segmentation allows businesses to customize their products, services, and marketing efforts based on location. By understanding how customer preferences and market conditions vary by geography, companies can optimize their strat.

Chapter 10: Developing a Logistics and Operations Plan

Developing a **logistics and operations plan** is essential for ensuring that a business runs smoothly and efficiently. These plans outline how a company will manage its supply chain, production processes, and overall operations to meet customer demand and achieve business goals. While logistics focuses on the movement and storage of goods, an operations plan covers the broader aspects of managing daily activities, resources, and workflows. Together, these plans help businesses streamline their processes, reduce costs, and improve customer satisfaction by ensuring timely delivery of products and services.

A comprehensive logistics and operations plan provides the blueprint for how products and services will be produced, stored, and delivered to customers. It ensures that every step of the supply chain and operational process is well-coordinated, from sourcing raw materials to shipping the final product. By having a well-defined plan in place, businesses can better manage risks, optimize resource allocation, and improve overall efficiency.

What is a Logistics Plan?

A **logistics plan** is a detailed outline that defines how a business will manage the flow of goods, services, and information from the point of origin to the point of consumption. It involves coordinating the movement, storage, and transportation of products, as well as managing inventory and ensuring that the right products are available at the right time to meet customer demand.

The logistics plan is a critical component of the supply chain, ensuring that all logistical operations—from sourcing materials to delivering finished goods—are efficient and cost-effective. For example, a retail company might need to coordinate the transportation of products from multiple suppliers to distribution centers and then to stores or directly to customers. A well-organized logistics plan ensures that these processes run smoothly, reducing delays, minimizing costs, and improving customer satisfaction.

Key elements of a logistics plan include:

- **Transportation**: Choosing the most efficient modes of transportation (e.g., trucks, ships, planes) to move goods between suppliers, warehouses, and customers.
- **Warehousing**: Managing storage facilities to ensure that inventory is stored safely and can be accessed easily when needed. This includes deciding how many warehouses are needed and where they should be located.
- **Inventory management**: Ensuring that stock levels are optimized to meet demand without overstocking, which ties up capital, or understocking, which leads to missed sales opportunities.

- **Order fulfillment**: Managing the process of picking, packing, and shipping products to customers. This includes ensuring that orders are processed quickly and accurately.

By developing an efficient logistics plan, businesses can reduce shipping costs, minimize lead times, and improve the overall customer experience. It also allows companies to respond more quickly to changes in demand or supply chain disruptions, providing greater flexibility and resilience.

Why Have a Logistics Plan?

Having a **logistics plan** is critical for several reasons. First and foremost, it ensures that the supply chain operates efficiently, minimizing delays and reducing costs. Without a clear logistics plan, businesses risk facing issues such as stock shortages, late deliveries, and higher transportation costs, all of which can negatively impact customer satisfaction and profitability.

A logistics plan helps businesses:
- **Optimize costs**: By carefully planning transportation routes, warehousing locations, and inventory levels, businesses can reduce unnecessary expenses. For example, a company can save money by choosing the most cost-effective shipping options or by consolidating shipments to reduce the number of deliveries required.

- **Improve customer service**: Fast and reliable delivery is a key factor in customer satisfaction. A well-designed logistics plan ensures that products are delivered on time and in good condition, which can enhance the customer experience and build brand loyalty.
- **Enhance flexibility**: In today's fast-paced business environment, supply chain disruptions can happen at any time. Whether it's a natural disaster, a supplier issue, or an unexpected surge in demand, having a logistics plan allows businesses to react quickly and make adjustments as needed. For example, if a primary transportation route is blocked, the logistics plan should outline alternative routes or backup suppliers to avoid delays.
- **Ensure scalability**: As a business grows, its logistics needs will evolve. A logistics plan allows companies to scale their operations efficiently by providing a roadmap for expanding warehousing capacity, increasing transportation capabilities, or managing larger volumes of orders.

In addition to these benefits, a well-organized logistics plan helps businesses maintain control over their supply chain, ensuring that products flow smoothly from suppliers to customers. It also helps businesses forecast demand more accurately, manage inventory levels more effectively, and allocate resources where they are most needed.

What is an Operations Plan?

An **operations plan** is a comprehensive document that outlines how a business will conduct its day-to-day activities to achieve its goals. It provides a detailed guide for managing resources, workflows, and processes across various departments, including production, human resources, marketing, and customer service. An operations plan focuses on the **internal workings** of the business, ensuring that each department is aligned with the company's overall strategy and objectives.

The primary purpose of an operations plan is to ensure that the business runs efficiently and consistently. This includes defining the tasks and responsibilities of each team, setting timelines for key activities, and allocating resources—such as personnel, equipment, and materials—needed to complete those tasks. For example, a manufacturing company's operations plan might outline the daily production schedule, the maintenance of machinery, and the staffing requirements needed to meet production targets.

Key components of an operations plan include:
- **Processes**: The specific steps or activities that need to be completed to deliver products or services to customers. This might include production schedules, quality control procedures, or customer service workflows.
- **Resources**: The materials, labor, and equipment required to carry out the business's activities. For example, a restaurant's operations plan might detail the number of staff needed during peak hours, the ingredients required for the menu, and the kitchen equipment maintenance schedule.

- **Timeline**: Setting clear deadlines for tasks and projects ensures that the business remains on track to meet its goals. This also helps employees manage their time effectively and prioritize critical activities.

An effective operations plan provides structure and accountability, ensuring that all departments work together to achieve the company's goals. It also helps businesses manage their resources efficiently, improve productivity, and reduce operational costs.

Writing an Operations Plan in Actions and Tasks

When **writing an operations plan**, it's essential to break down the business's goals into specific **actions and tasks** that can be assigned, tracked, and completed. This approach ensures that every part of the business has a clear understanding of what needs to be done and how it contributes to the overall objectives.

To write an operations plan effectively:

1. **Define clear objectives**: The operations plan should be based on the company's strategic goals. For example, if the business aims to increase production by 20% over the next year, the operations plan should outline the steps needed to achieve this goal, such as hiring additional staff, expanding facilities, or upgrading equipment.

2. **Assign responsibilities**: Each task in the operations plan should be assigned to a specific team or individual. Clear accountability ensures that there are no gaps in responsibility and that everyone knows what is expected of them. For example, the production manager might be responsible for overseeing daily output, while the HR department handles staffing and recruitment.
3. **Create detailed workflows**: Break down complex activities into smaller, manageable tasks. This helps ensure that each part of the process is completed in a logical order and that no steps are missed. For instance, in a manufacturing business, the operations plan might include a step-by-step workflow for assembling products, conducting quality control checks, and packaging the final product for shipment.
4. **Set timelines and milestones**: Establish deadlines for each task and set milestones to track progress. For example, if the goal is to launch a new product by the end of the year, the operations plan should include a timeline for product development, testing, marketing, and distribution.
5. **Monitor and adjust**: Operations plans should be dynamic and flexible, allowing for adjustments as needed. Regular reviews of the plan's progress help identify any issues early and make necessary changes to keep the business on track.

In conclusion, writing an operations plan in actions and tasks ensures that the business can function efficiently and effectively, with clear guidance on what needs to be done, who is responsible, and when tasks need to be completed. By breaking down the business's strategic goals into actionable steps, companies can ensure that they are well-positioned to meet customer demand, scale operations, and achieve long-term success.

Chapter 11: Creating a Profitable Financial Plan

A **financial plan** is the backbone of any successful business, guiding the company's decisions regarding investments, growth strategies, and daily operations. Creating a **profitable financial plan** means not only projecting future revenues and expenses but also ensuring that the business remains financially sustainable in both the short and long term. A well-crafted financial plan helps businesses allocate resources efficiently, manage risks, and assess the viability of their goals.

A comprehensive financial plan typically includes projected revenue, operating expenses, cash flow forecasts, and a breakdown of financial goals. More importantly, it involves the proper preparation and analysis of financial statements, such as the **Income Statement**, **Balance Sheet**, and **Cash Flow Statement**. These documents help monitor the business's performance and identify areas for improvement. By integrating **Key Performance Indicators (KPIs)** into the financial analysis, businesses can better understand profitability, solvency, and liquidity—critical metrics for maintaining financial health.

Proper Preparation of the Financial Statements

Proper preparation of **financial statements** is essential for maintaining transparency, making informed decisions, and attracting potential investors or lenders. The three primary financial statements—**Income Statement**, **Balance Sheet**, and **Cash Flow Statement**—offer a complete picture of a company's financial position.

1. **Income Statement (Profit and Loss Statement)**: This statement outlines the company's revenues, expenses, and profits over a specific period. The income statement provides an overview of how well the business is generating revenue relative to its costs. Key elements include gross revenue (sales), operating expenses (like wages, rent, and utilities), and net income (the company's profit after all expenses are deducted). Proper preparation ensures that each revenue and expense category is clearly defined and accurately recorded, giving a true reflection of the business's financial performance.
2. **Balance Sheet**: The balance sheet provides a snapshot of the company's assets, liabilities, and equity at a specific point in time. It reflects the company's financial stability by showing what it owns (assets) versus what it owes (liabilities). Assets can include cash, accounts receivable, and inventory, while liabilities might consist of loans, accounts payable, and other obligations. The balance sheet helps assess the company's ability to cover its debts and fund future growth, offering insight into its long-term financial health.

3. **Cash Flow Statement**: This statement tracks the flow of cash in and out of the business, categorized into operating, investing, and financing activities. Cash flow is critical for ensuring that the business can meet its financial obligations, pay employees, and invest in growth opportunities. A positive cash flow indicates that the business is generating enough money to cover its expenses and continue operations.

Each of these statements provides vital information about the company's financial health. Properly preparing and regularly reviewing these financial statements ensures that the business remains profitable and capable of achieving its long-term goals.

The Income Statement, the Balance Sheet, and Calculation of Profit or Loss

The **Income Statement**, also known as the Profit and Loss (P&L) statement, is the primary tool for calculating **profit or loss**. It summarizes the revenues earned and expenses incurred over a particular period, typically a quarter or a year. The goal is to determine whether the business is operating at a profit or a loss by subtracting total expenses from total revenues.

The **income statement** consists of:
- **Revenue**: The total amount of money generated from sales or services.
- **Cost of Goods Sold (COGS)**: The direct costs associated with producing the goods or services sold.
- **Gross Profit**: Calculated by subtracting COGS from total revenue, it reflects the profitability of the company's core activities.
- **Operating Expenses**: These include fixed and variable costs such as salaries, rent, utilities, and marketing.
- **Net Income (or Net Profit)**: The final profit or loss after all expenses, taxes, and interest are deducted. A positive net income indicates a profit, while a negative figure indicates a loss.

The **Balance Sheet** offers a more static view of the company's financial situation, detailing assets, liabilities, and equity at a specific moment. The formula for the balance sheet is:
- **Assets = Liabilities + Equity**.

Assets represent everything the company owns, from cash and equipment to inventory and property. Liabilities include loans, accounts payable, and other obligations. **Equity** reflects the residual value of the company after liabilities are subtracted from assets, essentially representing the shareholders' stake in the company. The balance sheet is used to assess a company's **solvency**—its ability to meet long-term financial commitments.

The **calculation of profit or loss** is a simple process of subtracting total expenses from total revenue:
- **Profit/Loss = Total Revenue - Total Expenses**.

If the result is positive, the business is profitable. If negative, the business is operating at a loss, requiring immediate adjustments to either increase revenue or reduce costs.

Reclassification of the Financial Statements into Key Performance Indicators

Reclassifying financial statements into **Key Performance Indicators (KPIs)** helps businesses track their performance in a more actionable way. KPIs are specific metrics that give insight into areas such as profitability, efficiency, liquidity, and solvency. By reclassifying financial data, companies can focus on the numbers that matter most to their operations and make more informed decisions.

Common KPIs derived from financial statements include:

- **Gross Profit Margin**: This KPI measures the percentage of revenue that exceeds the cost of goods sold (COGS). It indicates how efficiently the company is producing and selling its products. It is calculated as:
    - **Gross Profit Margin = (Gross Profit / Revenue) × 100**.
- **Net Profit Margin**: This metric shows how much of each dollar of revenue is profit after all expenses are deducted. It's a key indicator of overall profitability:
    - **Net Profit Margin = (Net Income / Revenue) × 100**.
- **Current Ratio**: This liquidity ratio assesses a company's ability to meet short-term obligations with its current assets:
    - **Current Ratio = Current Assets / Current Liabilities**.
- **Debt-to-Equity Ratio**: This solvency ratio measures the proportion of debt used to finance the company's assets compared to equity. A high ratio may indicate higher financial risk:

- **Debt-to-Equity Ratio = Total Liabilities / Shareholder Equity**.
- **Return on Investment (ROI)**: This measures how effectively a company uses its capital to generate profit. It's calculated as:
  - **ROI = (Net Profit / Total Investment) × 100**.

By using KPIs, businesses can better understand their financial position, track performance over time, and identify areas for improvement. KPIs allow for continuous monitoring and adjustment, ensuring that the company stays on track to meet its financial goals.

Definition of Accounting Principles: Profitability, Solvency, Liquidity

Understanding the core **accounting principles—profitability, solvency, and liquidity**—is critical for assessing a company's financial health and long-term viability.

1. **Profitability**: This principle measures a company's ability to generate more revenue than its expenses over time. Profitability is a key indicator of a company's success and growth potential. Profit margins (both gross and net) are commonly used to assess profitability. A profitable business is one that can sustainably generate income that exceeds its operating costs, ensuring long-term success and the ability to reinvest in growth.
2. **Solvency**: Solvency refers to a company's ability to meet its long-term financial obligations. A solvent company has enough assets to cover its liabilities, making it financially stable and less likely to face bankruptcy. The debt-to-equity ratio is a common measure of solvency, helping businesses understand how much of their operations are funded by debt versus equity. Maintaining a healthy solvency ratio is crucial for long-term financial stability and for securing loans or attracting investors.

3. **Liquidity**: Liquidity measures a company's ability to meet short-term obligations, such as paying bills, salaries, or suppliers. A company with good liquidity can quickly convert its assets into cash to cover these immediate expenses. Common liquidity ratios include the **current ratio** and **quick ratio**, which compare current assets to current liabilities. High liquidity ensures that a company can handle short-term financial challenges without needing to take on additional debt.

By mastering these accounting principles, businesses can maintain a solid financial foundation, make informed decisions, and plan for both short-term and long-term growth. These principles also play a vital role in creating a profitable financial plan that aligns with the company's strategic objectives and ensures financial sustainability.

In conclusion, a **profitable financial plan** is essential for maintaining a healthy, growing business. Proper preparation of financial statements, analyzing profitability through the income statement and balance sheet, using KPIs for continuous performance monitoring, and adhering to core accounting principles of profitability, solvency, and liquidity all contribute to the financial stability of the company.

What is a Financial Plan

A **financial plan** is a comprehensive outline that details a business's financial objectives, strategies, and projections for achieving profitability and sustainability. It serves as a roadmap for managing a company's finances, helping to guide decisions related to investments, operational costs, revenue generation, and growth. A financial plan typically includes income forecasts, expense budgets, cash flow projections, and key financial ratios, providing a clear picture of the company's current financial health and its anticipated future performance.

The primary components of a financial plan include:
- **Revenue Projections**: Estimating future sales based on market trends, customer demand, and historical data.
- **Expense Budgets**: Outlining both fixed and variable costs, such as rent, salaries, utilities, and raw materials.
- **Cash Flow Projections**: Predicting the inflows and outflows of cash to ensure the business has enough liquidity to cover short-term obligations.
- **Profit and Loss Statements**: Estimating profits by comparing projected revenues to expected expenses.
- **Break-Even Analysis**: Determining the point at which total revenue equals total expenses, meaning the business starts to generate a profit.
- **Capital Requirements**: Identifying the funds needed for investments, expansion, or day-to-day operations.

A financial plan helps businesses prepare for both expected and unexpected financial challenges. It provides the framework for evaluating whether the business has sufficient resources to meet its objectives and whether adjustments are necessary to stay on track. Regular updates to the financial plan are essential as market conditions and business needs change over time.

Why You Need a Financial Plan

A **financial plan** is essential for the success and sustainability of any business, regardless of its size or industry. Without a well-structured financial plan, businesses can face challenges such as cash flow shortages, misallocation of resources, and lack of direction in achieving profitability. The primary reason a business needs a financial plan is to provide **clarity and guidance** on how financial resources will be managed to achieve short-term and long-term objectives.

One of the key benefits of having a financial plan is that it helps businesses **anticipate future needs and challenges**. For example, a growing company might project that it will need additional funds for hiring, product development, or market expansion in the next year. With a financial plan in place, the company can prepare for these future expenses, seek financing if necessary, or adjust its spending to ensure it remains solvent. Similarly, businesses can use the plan to forecast potential risks, such as market downturns or supply chain disruptions, and develop strategies to mitigate them.

A financial plan is also critical for **securing investment and financing**. Investors, lenders, and financial institutions require a detailed financial plan to assess the viability and profitability of the business before providing funding. A solid financial plan demonstrates that the business has a clear strategy for generating revenue, managing expenses, and achieving profitability. It shows that the business is prepared to make sound financial decisions and use resources efficiently, increasing investor confidence. Additionally, a financial plan helps business owners and managers **make informed decisions**. By regularly reviewing financial projections and actual performance, companies can adjust their strategies to improve profitability, reduce costs, and optimize cash flow. It serves as a tool for measuring progress and ensures that the business remains aligned with its financial goals.

In conclusion, a financial plan is indispensable for effective financial management, future planning, and securing funding. It provides a clear, actionable roadmap that guides a business through financial challenges and helps it achieve long-term success.

Chapter 12: Defining the Management Organizational Structure (Organizational Chart)

A well-defined **management organizational structure** is critical for the efficient operation of any business. It outlines how the company is organized, who reports to whom, and the roles and responsibilities of each team member. An effective organizational structure ensures that the business runs smoothly, with clear communication channels, accountability, and authority distribution. The **organizational chart** is a visual representation of this structure, showing how different departments, teams, and individuals are interconnected.

A good management structure clarifies leadership roles, improves decision-making, and enhances productivity by ensuring that everyone knows their position and responsibilities within the organization. For companies of all sizes, the organizational structure helps to establish a clear chain of command, define authority levels, and streamline business processes.

Designing an Organizational Chart

Designing an organizational chart involves visually mapping out the hierarchy and functional relationships within a business. This chart serves as a blueprint for how different parts of the company interact and collaborate. It typically starts with the CEO or founder at the top, followed by senior executives, department heads, and employees.

The organizational chart helps to clarify the reporting structure and illustrates how each department supports the business's overall goals. When designing an organizational chart, several key considerations come into play:

- **Hierarchy**: The chart should represent the levels of authority within the company. Each person should know who they report to and who reports to them. For instance, the CEO may have direct reports such as a Chief Financial Officer (CFO), Chief Marketing Officer (CMO), and Chief Operations Officer (COO). These executives, in turn, manage various department heads who oversee specific teams, such as finance, marketing, or operations.
- **Departments**: The chart should group employees based on departments or functions, such as marketing, sales, HR, and product development. Each department should have a clear leader, like a department manager or director, responsible for overseeing day-to-day operations and ensuring that the team meets its objectives.

- **Flow of Communication**: The chart should depict formal lines of communication. Employees need to know who they can consult for decisions or problem-solving, ensuring that information flows smoothly across different levels of the organization. Designing the chart with a clear communication flow prevents bottlenecks and inefficiencies in decision-making.

In some businesses, the organizational structure may be **flat**, meaning fewer layers of management exist, which allows for more direct communication between executives and staff. In other cases, particularly in large organizations, the structure may be **hierarchical** or **divisional**, where multiple layers of management exist, each with its own area of responsibility. The design of the organizational chart should reflect the specific needs of the business and its growth stage.

By designing an organizational chart that reflects the company's goals and structure, management can ensure that there is clarity around roles, responsibilities, and decision-making authority. This clarity helps improve efficiency and allows the business to scale more effectively.

Who Does What

The "Who Does What" approach is fundamental to defining the **roles and responsibilities** of each member of the team. It helps create clarity within the organization by assigning specific tasks and ensuring that everyone understands their duties. This approach is particularly important as it prevents overlap in responsibilities, reduces confusion, and ensures accountability.

Each role within the organizational chart should have a clearly defined **job description** that outlines key responsibilities, daily tasks, and performance expectations. For example:

- **The CEO** is responsible for the overall direction of the company, setting strategic goals, managing investor relations, and ensuring long-term growth.
- **The CFO** manages the company's financial health, including budgeting, financial planning, reporting, and ensuring compliance with financial regulations.
- **The COO** oversees daily operations, ensuring that business processes run smoothly and efficiently.
- **Department Heads** (like Marketing, Sales, or Operations) are responsible for overseeing their teams, setting departmental goals, and managing resources within their areas of expertise.

Additionally, the "Who Does What" approach extends to every level of the company. For instance, within the marketing team, individual responsibilities should be clearly defined:

- **The Marketing Manager** oversees the entire marketing strategy, manages campaigns, and monitors KPIs.
- **The Content Strategist** is responsible for content creation and management, ensuring alignment with the company's marketing objectives.

- **The Social Media Manager** handles all social platforms, engages with customers online, and promotes the company's products and services.

Assigning specific roles ensures that each employee understands their function within the organization, reducing the risk of overlapping duties or missed tasks. It also helps management track performance and accountability by linking specific responsibilities to measurable outcomes.

Moreover, clearly defining roles is critical for **collaboration**. Knowing "who does what" ensures that teams can collaborate effectively across departments, especially on projects that involve multiple areas of expertise, such as product launches, marketing campaigns, or customer service initiatives.

When and Where

When and where activities and decisions take place within the organization is another crucial aspect of an effective management structure. It refers to setting **timelines and locations** for tasks and ensuring that the organizational structure supports efficient communication and decision-making processes.
In many companies, different departments and teams may operate across various locations or time zones, especially with the increasing prevalence of remote work. A clear organizational structure needs to define:
- **Where teams are located**: Whether employees work in-office, remotely, or in hybrid environments, the structure should address how to coordinate work across these spaces. For example, a remote IT department may operate in a different region than the marketing team, necessitating digital collaboration tools and flexible communication schedules.
- **When decisions are made**: Timely decision-making is critical to a company's success. For example, a weekly executive meeting may be set to address high-level strategic decisions, while daily team stand-ups help manage ongoing projects. Establishing these regular checkpoints ensures that the flow of information and decision-making keeps the company moving forward.

By clearly defining when and where activities take place, businesses can ensure that processes are efficient, reducing delays and improving the speed of decision-making. This also improves cross-functional coordination and ensures that the right people are involved at the right time in key decisions.

With Whom

The **"with whom"** element of the organizational structure focuses on collaboration and communication across teams, departments, and hierarchical levels. It clarifies **who needs to work together** to accomplish business objectives and ensures that everyone involved is aware of their role in the process. Cross-functional collaboration is essential for large projects and strategic initiatives. For example, launching a new product may involve collaboration between the marketing, sales, product development, and finance teams. Each department has its specific role:
- **Marketing** promotes the product.
- **Sales** converts leads into customers.
- **Product Development** ensures the product meets market demands.
- **Finance** manages the budget and forecasts revenue.

In this case, clear communication between departments is essential to ensure a successful product launch. Without proper coordination, the efforts of one team might not align with the others, resulting in delays or inconsistencies.

The organizational chart should also define **who interacts with external stakeholders**, such as investors, clients, suppliers, and partners. For example, the sales team may have regular interactions with customers, while senior executives manage relationships with investors. By defining these roles clearly, the company can streamline communication with external parties and ensure that there is consistency in how relationships are managed.

Which Responsibilities to Assign to the Team / Hierarchy

Assigning the right **responsibilities to the team** and its hierarchy is key to ensuring that tasks are completed efficiently and that the business operates smoothly. Each member of the organization must have clear, defined responsibilities aligned with their skills and the overall business strategy.

- **Senior management**: Responsible for setting the company's vision and strategic goals, senior managers oversee the high-level operations of the business. They focus on long-term planning, financial management, and stakeholder relations. The CEO, CFO, COO, and other executives form the backbone of the strategic leadership team.
- **Mid-level management**: Department heads and managers oversee daily operations in their respective areas. Their responsibilities include setting goals for their teams, ensuring that tasks are completed on time, and managing budgets and resources. They act as the bridge between senior management and operational staff.
- **Operational staff**: The employees who carry out the day-to-day tasks that keep the business running, such as customer service representatives, salespeople, marketing staff, and production workers. Their responsibilities are typically more focused and task-oriented, and they report to department heads or managers.

By assigning the right responsibilities at each level of the hierarchy, businesses ensure that there is accountability at every step. Clear responsibility assignments prevent confusion, ensure that tasks are completed on time, and support efficient resource management.

In conclusion, defining the management organizational structure through an organizational chart, assigning roles, and clarifying responsibilities are essential for a company's growth and success. A well-organized structure helps improve communication, accountability, and efficiency, ensuring that every team member understands their role in achieving the company's objectives.

Chapter 13 : Final Draft of a Business Plan for Potential Third-Party Investors

How to Create a Financial Plan Presentation

A **financial plan presentation** is a core component of your business plan, providing a snapshot of the financial health and future projections of your company. It's not just a collection of numbers but a strategic narrative that tells investors how their money will be used, how it will generate returns, and why your business is a sound investment. The presentation should be clear, concise, and visually compelling. Here are the essential steps to creating an effective financial plan presentation for potential investors:

1. Executive Summary

The executive summary is the most important section of your financial plan presentation. Investors often have limited time and review numerous business plans, so your summary should quickly grab their attention and encourage them to dive deeper into your business. The executive summary should briefly cover:
- **Company overview**: What does your business do?
- **Mission and vision**: What are your business goals and values?
- **Market opportunity**: What gap in the market does your business fill?

- **Financial highlights**: Provide a snapshot of key financial metrics, such as projected revenue, profit margins, and cash flow.
- **Investment opportunity**: Clearly state how much funding you're seeking and how it will be used.

For example, if you're launching an e-commerce platform for sustainable products, your executive summary might focus on the growing demand for eco-friendly goods and how your platform addresses that demand. The financial highlights should give investors an immediate sense of your revenue projections and profitability.

2. Financial Statements Overview

Presenting your **financial statements** clearly and accurately is essential. Investors need to see that your business is financially sound and has the potential to grow. Include the following key financial statements:

- **Income Statement (Profit and Loss Statement)**: This shows your revenue, costs, and profit over a specific period. Investors will look for trends in profitability and cost management.
- **Balance Sheet**: The balance sheet provides a snapshot of your company's assets, liabilities, and shareholders' equity. Investors use this to assess the financial stability and liquidity of your business.
- **Cash Flow Statement**: Cash flow is critical for any business, especially startups. This statement shows how cash moves in and out of the business, highlighting your ability to cover expenses and invest in growth.

Make sure to provide **projections** for these financial statements over the next three to five years, including assumptions about revenue growth, cost management, and market conditions. The projections should be based on realistic assumptions and supported by data from market research or historical performance.

3. Break-Even Analysis

The **break-even analysis** is a crucial part of your financial plan presentation. It shows investors the point at which your business will become profitable—when total revenues equal total costs. This analysis is particularly important for startups, as it helps investors understand how much revenue you need to generate to cover your fixed and variable costs.

To calculate the break-even point, you need to understand the following:

- **Fixed costs**: These are the costs that remain constant regardless of sales volume, such as rent, salaries, and utilities.
- **Variable costs**: These fluctuate based on production and sales levels, such as raw materials and packaging.
- **Sales price per unit**: The price at which you sell your product or service.
- **Contribution margin**: The difference between the sales price and the variable cost per unit.

Presenting this information in a clear graph or table will help investors quickly grasp how soon they can expect your business to become profitable and how much risk is involved.

4. Sales Forecast

A **sales forecast** is a projection of how much revenue your business expects to generate over a certain period, usually three to five years. This section is critical because it helps investors understand the potential for growth and profitability. Your sales forecast should be realistic, based on data from market research, historical sales (if applicable), and industry trends.

To create a detailed sales forecast, consider the following:

- **Customer segments**: Break down your forecast by different customer groups to show how each segment will contribute to overall sales.
- **Products or services**: Provide projections for each product or service line.
- **Pricing strategy**: Show how your pricing will impact sales volume and revenue.
- **Sales channels**: Include information on your distribution strategy (e.g., online, retail stores) and how each channel will contribute to sales.

Visual aids like graphs, charts, and tables can make your sales forecast more accessible and engaging for investors. Be prepared to explain the assumptions behind your projections, as investors will want to ensure they are grounded in reality.

5. Use of Funds

This section details **how you will allocate the funds** you are seeking from investors. Be specific and transparent about how much you need and how it will be used. Common uses of funds include:

- **Product development**: Expanding or improving your product or service offering.
- **Marketing and sales**: Increasing brand awareness, customer acquisition, or expanding sales efforts.
- **Operations**: Hiring new employees, upgrading technology, or improving production processes.
- **Expansion**: Opening new locations or entering new markets.

Investors want to know that their money will be used effectively to drive growth and generate returns. By providing a clear breakdown of your funding needs, you demonstrate that you have a strategic plan for using the capital to achieve business milestones.

6. Risk Analysis
No investment is without risk, and investors will want to know what challenges your business might face and how you plan to mitigate them. A thorough **risk analysis** shows that you have carefully considered potential obstacles and have strategies in place to address them. Common risks to consider include:
- **Market risk**: Changes in consumer demand, competition, or economic conditions that could affect sales.
- **Operational risk**: Issues related to supply chain management, production delays, or staffing challenges.
- **Financial risk**: Cash flow shortages, difficulty securing additional funding, or rising costs.
- **Regulatory risk**: Legal or compliance issues that could impact your business operations.

After identifying potential risks, explain your **risk mitigation strategies**. For example, if you're concerned about market risk, you might highlight plans to diversify your product line or enter new markets to reduce dependency on a single revenue stream.

7. Exit Strategy
Investors will want to know how they can **exit the investment** and realize a return on their capital. Your exit strategy could include:
- **Acquisition**: Being acquired by a larger company.
- **Initial Public Offering (IPO)**: Taking the company public by offering shares on the stock market.
- **Mergers**: Merging with another company to increase market share or enter new markets.
- **Share buyback**: Buying back shares from investors after reaching profitability.

An exit strategy reassures investors that you have thought about their long-term interests and how they can potentially make a profit from investing in your business.

Why You Need a Financial Plan Presentation

A **financial plan presentation** is essential for several reasons. It not only provides potential investors with the information they need to assess the viability of your business but also demonstrates that you have a clear understanding of your company's financial health and future potential. Here's why a well-prepared financial plan presentation is critical:

1. To Secure Funding

One of the primary reasons for creating a financial plan presentation is to secure funding from investors. Whether you're seeking venture capital, angel investment, or loans from financial institutions, investors will expect a thorough and professional financial presentation that demonstrates your business's potential to grow and generate returns. By presenting detailed financial statements, forecasts, and a clear use of funds, you build trust with investors and increase the likelihood of receiving the capital you need to grow your business.

A compelling financial plan presentation shows that you understand your market, have realistic growth expectations, and have a well-thought-out strategy for using investor funds efficiently.

2. To Demonstrate Financial Health

Investors want to see that your business is financially healthy or has the potential to become profitable. A financial plan presentation that includes profit and loss projections, cash flow analysis, and a strong balance sheet demonstrates your company's financial stability. It also shows that you have a solid understanding of how to manage your finances effectively.

Investors will look for trends in your financials—such as increasing revenue, controlled expenses, and improving margins—that suggest your business is on a path to profitability. A thorough financial plan reassures investors that their investment is relatively low risk and likely to generate returns over time.

3. To Provide Transparency

Transparency is critical when dealing with potential investors. A well-prepared financial plan presentation offers a clear and honest view of your company's financial position, its challenges, and its opportunities. Investors appreciate transparency because it allows them to make informed decisions based on accurate data.

In your presentation, address potential risks and how you plan to mitigate them. Be honest about any weaknesses in your financials and explain the steps you're taking to improve your company's performance. This openness builds trust with investors, increasing the chances that they will invest in your business.

4. To Align Business Goals and Financial Projections

A financial plan presentation helps align your **business goals** with your **financial projections**. Investors want to see that your financials support your overall business strategy. For example, if you plan to expand into new markets or launch new products, your financial plan should include the costs associated with these initiatives and the expected return on investment.

By linking your business goals to your financial projections, you show investors that you have a clear plan for growth and that you're making decisions based on sound financial principles. This alignment strengthens your credibility and demonstrates that your business has a solid foundation for achieving its long-term objectives.

5. To Establish Credibility and Confidence

A well-prepared financial plan presentation establishes your credibility as a business leader and instills confidence in potential investors. Investors want to work with entrepreneurs who understand their business inside and out, including the financial side. By presenting a detailed financial plan, you demonstrate that you have the expertise and foresight needed to grow the business successfully.

Moreover, a strong financial presentation indicates that you are serious about your business and are committed to making it profitable. This level of professionalism can differentiate your business from others competing for the same investment dollars.

6. To Set Realistic Expectations

Setting **realistic expectations** is crucial when presenting to investors. Overly optimistic financial projections can lead to disappointment and loss of investor trust if your business fails to meet those expectations. A solid financial plan presentation includes realistic revenue and profit forecasts, backed by market data, industry trends, and historical performance (if applicable).

By setting realistic expectations, you not only build trust with investors but also create a foundation for long-term relationships. Investors are more likely to continue supporting your business if they feel confident that your projections are achievable and that you have a plan to overcome challenges.

In conclusion, creating a **Final Draft of a Business Plan** with a strong **financial plan presentation** is critical for attracting potential third-party investors. This process involves more than just showing financial figures; it requires clearly explaining how your business will generate revenue, manage expenses, and grow over time. Investors need to see that you understand your market, have realistic growth expectations, and have a strategic plan for managing risks and achieving profitability.

By addressing key elements such as the **Executive Summary, Financial Statements, Break-Even Analysis, Sales Forecast, Use of Funds, Risk Analysis**, and **Exit Strategy**, you provide a comprehensive view of your business's financial health and potential for success. Additionally, a well-prepared financial plan presentation helps you build credibility, align business goals with financial projections, and set realistic expectations, all of which are critical for securing the investment needed to drive your business forward.

Chapter 14: Monitoring Key Financial Indicators

Effective business management requires a constant focus on **monitoring key financial indicators** to ensure the company remains on track toward achieving its goals. These indicators provide valuable insights into the health of a business, helping leaders make informed decisions about operations, investments, and growth. By regularly reviewing financial statements and reclassifying them into consistent financial indicators, businesses can better assess their profitability, solvency, and liquidity. This chapter explores how to translate financial data into actionable metrics, focusing on the **Income Statement**, **Balance Sheet**, and the reclassification of financial statements into essential performance indicators such as **ROS**, **ROI**, and **ROE**.

From Proper Preparation of the Financial Statements to Reclassification into Consistent Financial Indicators for Making Informed Managerial and Entrepreneurial Decisions

The starting point for **monitoring key financial indicators** is the accurate and timely preparation of financial statements. The **Income Statement**, **Balance Sheet**, and **Cash Flow Statement** provide a comprehensive overview of the company's financial health, but these documents alone may not give managers the full picture they need to make strategic decisions. To gain deeper insights, it's necessary to **reclassify financial statements** into specific indicators that measure performance across profitability, liquidity, and solvency.

For example, while an Income Statement shows overall profit or loss, it may not provide the full context for understanding **profitability ratios** like the **Return on Sales (ROS)**. Similarly, the Balance Sheet offers a snapshot of a company's assets and liabilities but doesn't directly convey metrics like the **Return on Equity (ROE)**, which can indicate how effectively the company is using shareholder capital to generate profit.

By reclassifying financial data into relevant financial indicators, companies can make more informed decisions regarding resource allocation, cost management, and investment opportunities. Financial indicators transform raw data into actionable intelligence, helping businesses identify areas for improvement and capitalize on growth opportunities. For instance, a low ROI might prompt management to reconsider its investment strategy, while strong ROS can signal that the company's sales strategy is performing well.

Moreover, these indicators allow for **comparative analysis** against industry benchmarks and competitors, giving businesses a clearer sense of where they stand in the market. This comparison is vital for identifying strengths and weaknesses and adjusting business strategies accordingly. Through proper reclassification and regular monitoring, financial indicators can become a powerful tool for driving long-term growth and sustainability.

The Company's Financial Statements: Income Statement and Balance Sheet

The **Income Statement** and **Balance Sheet** are the two most critical financial statements used to assess a company's performance. Each serves a unique purpose in helping business leaders and investors understand the company's financial position.

The **Income Statement** (or **Profit and Loss Statement**) reflects the company's profitability over a specific period, typically quarterly or annually. It outlines revenue earned, expenses incurred, and the net profit or loss. Key components include:

- **Revenue**: The total income generated from sales or services.
- **Cost of Goods Sold (COGS)**: The direct costs of producing goods or services.
- **Gross Profit**: The difference between revenue and COGS, indicating the company's efficiency in production.
- **Operating Expenses**: The costs of running the business, including salaries, rent, and utilities.
- **Net Profit (or Net Income)**: The bottom line that shows whether the company made a profit or incurred a loss.

The **Balance Sheet**, on the other hand, provides a snapshot of the company's financial position at a specific moment in time. It shows the relationship between a company's **assets**, **liabilities**, and **equity**, following the basic accounting equation: **Assets = Liabilities + Equity**.

- **Assets** include everything the company owns, such as cash, inventory, equipment, and property.
- **Liabilities** represent the company's obligations, including loans, accounts payable, and other debts.

- **Equity** reflects the ownership stake of shareholders and retained earnings.

Together, these statements give a detailed view of the company's **financial performance** (Income Statement) and **financial position** (Balance Sheet). While the Income Statement reveals how efficiently the business is operating and generating profit, the Balance Sheet shows the company's stability and ability to meet its obligations.

For managerial purposes, these financial statements must be continuously monitored and analyzed. However, to extract deeper insights, the raw data needs to be converted into **financial ratios** and performance indicators that provide a more granular view of the company's health.

Reclassification of Financial Statements into Indicators: ROS / ROI / ROE to Help Understand the Company's Economic and Financial Performance

Reclassifying financial statements into key indicators such as **ROS (Return on Sales)**, **ROI (Return on Investment)**, and **ROE (Return on Equity)** allows businesses to better assess their **economic and financial performance**. These indicators offer valuable insights into how efficiently a company is generating profits, utilizing investments, and rewarding shareholders.

- **Return on Sales (ROS):** This indicator measures **operational efficiency** by calculating the percentage of sales that result in profit. It is calculated as:
    - **ROS = (Net Profit / Revenue) × 100**. ROS provides insight into how well the company controls costs relative to its revenue. A higher ROS indicates that the company is efficiently converting sales into profits, while a lower ROS suggests the need to evaluate cost structures or pricing strategies. ROS is particularly important for businesses with tight margins, where small cost reductions can lead to significant improvements in profitability.
- **Return on Investment (ROI):** ROI assesses the **effectiveness of investments** in generating profits. It is calculated as:

- **ROI = (Net Profit / Total Investment) × 100**. ROI helps managers and investors determine whether an investment is yielding satisfactory returns compared to alternative investment opportunities. A low ROI might indicate inefficient use of resources, prompting a review of current investments or operational strategies. Monitoring ROI is critical for businesses looking to expand or launch new projects, as it reveals whether the capital invested is being used effectively.
- **Return on Equity (ROE):** This indicator measures how efficiently a company is using shareholders' equity to generate profit. It is calculated as:
  - **ROE = (Net Income / Shareholder's Equity) × 100**. ROE is a key metric for investors, as it shows how well the company is using their invested capital. A high ROE indicates strong performance and suggests that the company is generating high returns on the money shareholders have invested. Conversely, a low ROE may suggest inefficiencies in using capital, potentially signaling financial weaknesses.

By regularly calculating and monitoring ROS, ROI, and ROE, businesses can better understand their **financial health** and identify areas for improvement. These indicators offer a more dynamic and precise understanding of performance than financial statements alone, helping managers make informed decisions about investments, cost management, and profitability.

Monitoring Profitability, Solvency, and Liquidity

To maintain a healthy financial position, businesses must closely monitor their **profitability, solvency,** and **liquidity**. Each of these aspects provides a different perspective on the company's ability to operate efficiently, meet its obligations, and grow sustainably.

- **Profitability**: Profitability refers to the company's ability to generate income from its operations. Key metrics for measuring profitability include gross profit margin, operating profit margin, and net profit margin. **Profitability indicators** like ROS and ROE give insights into how well the company is converting revenue into profit and how efficiently it uses its assets and equity. Continuous monitoring of profitability ensures that the company can maintain its growth trajectory and reinvest in its operations without sacrificing financial health.
- **Solvency**: Solvency reflects the company's ability to meet its long-term financial obligations. A **solvency ratio** such as the **debt-to-equity ratio** helps assess whether the company has a healthy balance between debt and equity. A high debt-to-equity ratio might indicate financial risk, as the company is heavily reliant on borrowed capital. Monitoring solvency helps businesses avoid excessive leverage and ensures that they can continue operations even during economic downturns or unexpected disruptions.

- **Liquidity**: Liquidity refers to the company's ability to meet short-term obligations, such as paying suppliers, employees, or utilities. Key liquidity ratios include the **current ratio** (current assets divided by current liabilities) and the **quick ratio**, which excludes inventory from current assets. These ratios help businesses determine if they have enough liquid assets (such as cash and accounts receivable) to cover immediate liabilities. Maintaining good liquidity ensures that the company can continue operating smoothly without facing cash flow issues.

By monitoring these key indicators, businesses can proactively manage their **financial health**. Regularly reviewing profitability, solvency, and liquidity helps identify potential financial risks early on, enabling management to take corrective action before problems escalate. It also helps companies optimize their operational efficiency, ensuring long-term sustainability and growth.

In conclusion, **monitoring key financial indicators** is an ongoing process that transforms raw financial data into actionable insights. From preparing and reclassifying financial statements to calculating key ratios like **ROS**, **ROI**, and **ROE**, businesses can gain a clearer picture of their economic and financial performance. Regularly tracking **profitability**, **solvency**, and **liquidity** is essential for making informed decisions that drive long-term success, ensuring that the company remains competitive, stable, and profitable in an ever-changing market.

To Gain Deep Insights and Make the Best Strategic Decisions for the Future of the Business

Gaining **deep insights** into a company's operations, market trends, and financial health is critical for making **strategic decisions** that will ensure its future growth and sustainability. Deep insights allow business leaders to not only understand their current position but also anticipate potential opportunities and challenges. This level of understanding helps in crafting strategies that are data-driven, customer-focused, and aligned with long-term objectives.

To gain these insights, businesses must first establish robust systems for **data collection and analysis**. By leveraging modern analytics tools, companies can track customer behavior, identify market trends, and monitor internal processes in real time. This allows leadership to make decisions based on concrete data rather than intuition or guesswork. For example, data on customer preferences can guide product development, while insights into supply chain efficiency can help reduce costs or improve delivery times. Access to this level of granular information helps businesses react swiftly to changes in the market and stay ahead of competitors.

Moreover, deep insights are essential for understanding **market dynamics** and customer needs. A thorough market analysis can reveal shifts in consumer behavior, emerging trends, or new competitive threats. For instance, a business in the eyewear industry might notice an increasing demand for sustainable products. By gaining this insight early, the company can pivot to introduce eco-friendly eyewear options, positioning itself as a leader in this growing segment. Similarly, understanding customer pain points through feedback and data analysis can inform customer service improvements or product enhancements, fostering loyalty and long-term engagement.

Financial insights are equally important in strategic decision-making. Regularly analyzing **financial statements**—including the income statement, balance sheet, and cash flow—gives business leaders a clear picture of profitability, liquidity, and solvency. By reclassifying financial data into **Key Performance Indicators (KPIs)**, such as Return on Investment (ROI) or gross profit margin, companies can monitor their performance against benchmarks and industry standards. For example, tracking the ROI of different marketing campaigns helps identify which efforts deliver the highest return, allowing the company to allocate resources more efficiently in the future.

Additionally, **scenario analysis** is a powerful tool for gaining insights that lead to sound strategic decisions. By exploring different business scenarios—such as best-case, worst-case, and most-likely scenarios—leaders can prepare for various potential outcomes and develop contingency plans. This proactive approach reduces risks and enhances a company's ability to adapt to unforeseen changes in the market, such as economic downturns or supply chain disruptions.

Long-term strategic decisions also benefit from insights into **technological advancements**. Staying informed about new technologies that could impact the industry enables businesses to innovate and remain competitive. For example, in the e-commerce space, adopting artificial intelligence for personalized shopping experiences or using augmented reality to let customers virtually try on products can significantly enhance customer satisfaction and drive sales. Failing to keep pace with technological advancements, on the other hand, can leave a company behind its more innovative competitors.

Ultimately, gaining deep insights is about creating a **culture of continuous learning and adaptation**. Business leaders must foster an environment where data-driven decision-making is prioritized, and teams are encouraged to analyze their performance and look for ways to improve. This approach ensures that every strategic decision is informed by comprehensive insights, leading to more successful outcomes and a clearer path for future growth.

In conclusion, gaining deep insights is fundamental to making the best **strategic decisions** for the future of the business. These insights allow companies to understand their market, their customers, and their financial health, all of which are essential for navigating the complex business landscape and ensuring long-term success. By leveraging data and staying adaptable to change, companies can position themselves for sustained growth and resilience in the face of evolving market conditions.

To Establish Credibility with Third-Party Investors

Establishing **credibility with third-party investors** is essential for any business seeking external funding, whether from venture capitalists, angel investors, or financial institutions. Credibility not only reassures investors that the business is a sound investment but also helps foster long-term partnerships that can provide ongoing support and resources.
Demonstrating credibility involves a combination of transparent financial reporting, a clear strategic vision, strong leadership, and a track record of success or measurable progress.
One of the most important factors in establishing credibility with investors is **financial transparency**. Investors need to see that the business is managing its finances responsibly and has a clear plan for generating returns. This involves presenting **accurate and detailed financial statements**, including the income statement, balance sheet, and cash flow statement. By providing a transparent view of the company's current financial health, businesses can build trust with investors. Additionally, offering **financial forecasts** that are realistic and based on sound assumptions helps investors understand the company's growth potential. Forecasts should include revenue projections, profit margins, and a clear breakdown of how funds will be used to achieve business goals.
In addition to financial transparency, having a well-defined **strategic vision** is crucial for gaining investor confidence. Investors want to know that the company's leadership has a clear plan for the future and understands the steps needed to achieve long-term success. This includes articulating the company's

mission, outlining its target market, and explaining how the business plans to differentiate itself from competitors. For example, a company in the eyewear industry might present a strategy focused on expanding into international markets or launching a new line of eco-friendly products to capture the growing demand for sustainable goods. A well-thought-out strategic vision demonstrates to investors that the company is not only aware of its opportunities but is also prepared to capitalize on them.

Strong leadership is another critical factor in establishing credibility with third-party investors. Investors are placing their trust—and money—in the ability of the management team to execute the business plan and navigate challenges. A proven leadership team with a track record of success in the industry can significantly enhance a company's credibility. Even if the company is a startup without a long operational history, having leaders who have experience in growing businesses or have demonstrated expertise in key areas such as finance, marketing, or product development can reassure investors that the business is in capable hands.

Another important aspect of building credibility is **demonstrating traction** or measurable progress. Investors want to see that the business is already gaining momentum, whether through increasing sales, growing market share, or successfully launching new products. Highlighting **key milestones** that the company has achieved, such as reaching a certain number of customers, securing partnerships, or receiving positive customer feedback, shows investors that the business is on a promising trajectory. Even if the business is still in its early stages, demonstrating progress toward these goals provides evidence that the company has the potential to scale and generate returns on investment.

Chapter 15: Cash Flow Analysis

Cash flow analysis is a critical aspect of managing a business's finances and ensuring its long-term sustainability. While profitability is important, cash flow represents the actual movement of money in and out of the company, determining its ability to meet short-term obligations, reinvest in growth, and respond to unexpected expenses. Even a profitable business can struggle if it lacks adequate cash flow to cover immediate needs, making this analysis vital for both day-to-day operations and strategic planning.

A **cash flow analysis** focuses on three primary components: **operating activities**, **investing activities**, and **financing activities**. By breaking down cash inflows and outflows into these categories, businesses can gain a comprehensive understanding of their liquidity and overall financial health. Regular cash flow monitoring allows for proactive management, ensuring that the business has sufficient liquidity to operate efficiently and pursue growth opportunities without risking insolvency.

Liquidity Index Generated by the Business Activity

The **liquidity index** is a key metric in cash flow analysis, measuring how quickly a business can convert its assets into cash to cover short-term obligations. Unlike profitability ratios, which measure long-term success, the liquidity index focuses on a company's ability to remain operational on a day-to-day basis by maintaining an adequate flow of cash. This index is particularly important for businesses that have significant receivables or inventory but face immediate financial obligations, such as payroll, rent, or supplier payments.

The **liquidity index** is calculated by comparing a company's current assets—such as cash, accounts receivable, and inventory—to its current liabilities. Key liquidity ratios include:

- **Current Ratio**: This measures the company's ability to cover its short-term liabilities with its short-term assets. A current ratio of more than 1 indicates that the company has more assets than liabilities, suggesting that it is in a good liquidity position.
    - **Current Ratio = Current Assets / Current Liabilities**.
- **Quick Ratio (or Acid-Test Ratio)**: This is a more stringent measure of liquidity, excluding inventory from current assets to focus only on assets that can be quickly converted into cash. A high quick ratio means that the company can cover its liabilities even without selling its inventory.
    - **Quick Ratio = (Current Assets - Inventory) / Current Liabilities**.

Maintaining a healthy liquidity index is essential for **business continuity**. It ensures that the company can meet its short-term obligations without having to take on additional debt or sell long-term assets. A low liquidity index, on the other hand, can be a warning sign that the business may face difficulties in paying its bills, even if it is profitable on paper. Regularly monitoring this index helps businesses avoid liquidity crises and ensures that cash is available when needed.

Proper Management of Cash Flows

Proper **management of cash flows** involves carefully balancing cash inflows (money coming into the business) and cash outflows (money going out of the business). While the Income Statement measures profitability, cash flow management ensures that the business can meet its immediate financial needs. The key to managing cash flows effectively is to ensure that inflows consistently exceed outflows, or at the very least, that there is sufficient cash on hand to cover short-term obligations during periods of lower revenue.

Effective cash flow management focuses on optimizing both the **timing** and **volume** of cash movements. Businesses must ensure that they receive payments from customers promptly while controlling expenses and delaying payments to suppliers or creditors as needed without incurring penalties. Tools such as cash flow forecasts can help businesses anticipate periods of cash shortages or surpluses and plan accordingly.

A well-managed cash flow system provides several key benefits:

- **Improved liquidity**: Ensuring that there is enough cash on hand to meet short-term liabilities such as payroll, rent, and utilities.

- **Reduced financing costs**: Minimizing the need for short-term borrowing by maintaining healthy cash reserves.
- **Enhanced decision-making**: Knowing exactly how much cash is available allows businesses to make informed decisions about investments, purchases, and other expenditures.
- **Preparedness for emergencies**: Having a buffer of cash ensures that the company can handle unexpected expenses, such as equipment breakdowns, legal fees, or sudden drops in sales.

Proper cash flow management also allows businesses to **capitalize on opportunities**. For example, if a business has excess cash, it can use this surplus to take advantage of supplier discounts, invest in new technology, or expand operations. Conversely, businesses that do not manage their cash flows properly may miss out on such opportunities due to a lack of available funds.

Management of Cash Inflows

Effective management of **cash inflows** is essential for maintaining a steady flow of capital into the business. Cash inflows primarily come from operating activities, such as sales revenue, but can also include money from financing (e.g., loans or investments) and investing activities (e.g., selling assets). For most businesses, the main challenge is ensuring that cash inflows are consistent and sufficient to cover operational costs.

One of the key strategies for managing cash inflows is **optimizing the collection of receivables**. This involves ensuring that customers pay their invoices on time. Delayed payments can lead to cash flow shortages, forcing the business to rely on external financing or delay payments to its own suppliers. To avoid this, businesses can implement the following strategies:

- **Clear payment terms**: Establishing upfront, clear terms for payment (e.g., net 30 or net 60 days) helps set expectations for when payments are due.
- **Invoicing promptly**: Sending invoices immediately after goods or services are delivered ensures that customers are billed quickly, speeding up the collection process.
- **Incentives for early payments**: Offering small discounts for early payments can encourage customers to pay ahead of schedule, improving cash inflows.
- **Following up on overdue accounts**: Implementing a system for following up with customers who have overdue invoices helps reduce the risk of non-payment or late payment.

Another important aspect of managing cash inflows is **diversifying revenue streams**. Businesses that rely on a single product, service, or customer for a significant portion of their revenue are vulnerable to fluctuations in demand or payment delays. Diversifying into multiple products, services, or customer segments can help ensure a more stable and predictable flow of cash. Additionally, businesses should consider having a combination of short-term and long-term contracts to balance steady income with higher-margin, one-time projects.

Monitoring **cash flow forecasts** can help businesses predict upcoming inflows and manage expectations. By projecting future sales and payments, companies can plan for periods when cash inflows may be lower (e.g., seasonal businesses) and adjust their operations accordingly.

Management of Cash Outflows

Cash outflows, or the money leaving the business, must be managed just as carefully as inflows to maintain a healthy cash flow. Outflows include expenses like rent, salaries, utilities, supplier payments, loan repayments, and taxes. Properly managing these outflows ensures that the business does not run out of cash, even during periods of reduced revenue.

One of the most important aspects of managing cash outflows is **controlling costs**. Businesses should regularly review their expenses to identify areas where savings can be made without negatively affecting operations. Common strategies for controlling cash outflows include:

- **Negotiating with suppliers**: Businesses can often reduce their costs by negotiating better payment terms or bulk purchase discounts with

suppliers. For example, paying suppliers early might earn a discount, while negotiating longer payment terms can help businesses retain cash longer.
- **Outsourcing non-core functions**: Some companies can reduce costs by outsourcing functions such as IT, HR, or marketing. Outsourcing allows businesses to reduce overhead by paying for services only when needed, rather than maintaining full-time staff for these functions.
- **Implementing cost control measures**: Monitoring operational expenses closely and setting spending limits for departments can help prevent unnecessary outflows. For example, limiting travel expenses or cutting non-essential purchases during cash flow crunches can make a significant difference.

Another important strategy is **scheduling payments** to align with cash inflows. Businesses should aim to delay cash outflows without incurring penalties, allowing them to retain cash longer. For example, using the full payment period (e.g., 30 or 60 days) to pay suppliers helps the business keep more cash in hand, which can be used for short-term investments or to cover urgent expenses.

Managing **debt payments** is also critical. If a business has taken on loans or credit lines, it needs to carefully manage repayments to avoid penalties or interest. Refinancing debt at lower interest rates, consolidating loans, or adjusting repayment schedules can free up cash that would otherwise be tied up in debt servicing.

Proper management of cash outflows ensures that a business retains enough liquidity to operate efficiently, meet its financial obligations, and invest in growth opportunities. Businesses that fail to control their outflows may face cash shortages, forcing them to take on additional debt or reduce operations.

Bonus Chapter: Case Study: Luxor Incorporation Limited Liability CompanyCompany Founders: 4 Persons

The founding team of any company plays a pivotal role in setting the strategic direction and building the foundation for success. In this case, the company was founded by **four individuals**, each bringing a unique set of skills, expertise, and passion to the business. These founders are united by a shared vision and a commitment to solving an important global issue—caring for people's eye health while offering stylish and functional eyewear. Their diverse backgrounds in **business, technology, fashion, and healthcare** create a well-rounded leadership team capable of addressing the many challenges that come with building a successful e-commerce platform in the competitive eyewear market.

Each founder contributes a distinct strength to the company's growth:

1. **Founder 1: The Visionary Leader** – With extensive experience in the **fashion and retail** industry, this founder leads the company's product development and branding efforts. Their eye for design ensures that the company's sunglasses and eyeglass frames are not only high-quality but also stylish and appealing to a broad customer base. They are responsible for identifying market trends, curating product collections, and ensuring that the company stays ahead of fashion trends while maintaining a focus on functionality.

2. **Founder 2: The Operations Expert** – Specializing in **e-commerce logistics and supply chain management**, this founder handles the operational side of the business. From managing relationships with suppliers to overseeing the warehousing and distribution of products, they ensure that the company runs smoothly and efficiently. Their expertise allows the business to offer fast and reliable delivery to customers around the world, while also minimizing costs and maximizing profit margins.
3. **Founder 3: The Tech Guru** – As the driving force behind the company's **technology and digital platform**, this founder ensures that the e-commerce site is user-friendly, secure, and scalable. Their background in **software development** and **digital marketing** enables the company to provide a seamless online shopping experience, integrate advanced analytics, and optimize the customer journey. This founder is also responsible for the company's data-driven approach to customer engagement and targeted marketing efforts.
4. **Founder 4: The Healthcare Advocate** – With a strong background in **optometry** and **healthcare**, this founder brings a deep understanding of eye health and the importance of high-quality eyewear. They ensure that the company maintains a commitment to promoting eye care, working closely with manufacturers to ensure that all products meet industry standards for quality and comfort. This founder is also responsible for developing partnerships with eye health professionals and launching initiatives aimed at raising awareness about the importance of eye care.

Together, these four founders provide a strong foundation for the company, blending creativity, technical expertise, operational efficiency, and a deep commitment to improving global eye health.

Vision: Taking Care of People's Eyes Around the World

The company's **vision** is centered on a profound and universal goal: **"Taking Care of People's Eyes Around the World."** This vision reflects the founders' commitment to promoting better eye health by providing high-quality eyewear that not only enhances vision but also protects eyes from the harmful effects of UV radiation and prolonged screen exposure. The company aims to become a global leader in the eyewear industry by offering products that combine style, functionality, and eye care.

This vision is inspired by the growing need for accessible, high-quality eyewear as people around the world increasingly prioritize their eye health. With the rise of digital devices and longer screen time, there is a heightened awareness of the importance of protecting and caring for one's eyes. The company aims to address these challenges by offering products that cater to various needs—from fashion-forward sunglasses that provide UV protection to prescription eyeglass frames designed for comfort and durability.

The vision goes beyond just selling eyewear. The company aspires to create a lasting impact on global eye health by educating customers about the importance of regular eye check-ups, proper eye care practices, and the benefits of investing in quality eyewear. This is achieved through strategic partnerships with optometrists, eye care clinics, and health organizations, all aligned with the company's mission to promote better eye health.

By adopting a **global perspective**, the company is committed to expanding its reach to underserved markets where access to affordable and high-quality eyewear is limited. Whether through its online platform or partnerships with local distributors, the company aims to ensure that everyone, regardless of geographic location, has access to the products and information they need to protect their vision and enjoy a better quality of life.

Mission: E-commerce Platform to Sell High-Quality Sunglasses and Eyeglass Frames in the Mid-to-High Price Range

The company's **mission** is focused on building a **premium e-commerce platform** designed to sell **high-quality sunglasses and eyeglass frames** within the **mid-to-high price range**. This mission reflects the company's commitment to offering products that strike a balance between style, durability, and affordability. By positioning itself in the mid-to-high segment of the market, the company targets customers who value both quality and aesthetics in their eyewear but are also mindful of price.

The e-commerce platform is at the core of the company's strategy, providing a seamless, user-friendly shopping experience that allows customers to browse, compare, and purchase eyewear from the comfort of their homes. The platform is designed to offer a diverse selection of products, catering to a wide range of customer preferences, whether they are looking for classic, timeless frames or bold, fashion-forward designs. Each product is meticulously curated to ensure that it meets the company's high standards for quality, craftsmanship, and functionality.

In line with the mission to serve the mid-to-high price segment, the company emphasizes the use of premium materials—such as high-grade acetate, titanium, and polarized lenses—that provide both durability and comfort. The frames are designed to be lightweight yet sturdy, offering customers long-lasting value for their investment. Additionally, the company offers **customizable options**, such as prescription lenses and adjustable frame sizes, to ensure that customers receive a personalized product that meets their specific needs.

The e-commerce platform is also designed to **enhance customer engagement** through features such as virtual try-on tools, detailed product descriptions, customer reviews, and personalized recommendations. These features aim to replicate the in-store shopping experience, making it easy for customers to find the perfect pair of sunglasses or eyeglasses that suit their style and vision requirements. The company also places a strong emphasis on customer service, offering hassle-free returns, fast shipping, and responsive support to ensure a smooth and satisfying shopping experience. By focusing on the mid-to-high price range, the company aims to **differentiate itself** from both low-cost, mass-produced eyewear brands and ultra-luxury eyewear companies. The mission is to provide customers with high-quality, stylish eyewear that offers excellent value for money, combining premium materials and craftsmanship with competitive pricing.

A Global Vision for Eye Care and Fashion

The company's mission is not just about selling eyewear but also about creating a platform that serves as a **hub for eye care education** and fashion innovation. Through its e-commerce platform, the company aims to promote the idea that eyewear is not only a necessity for improving vision but also an essential fashion accessory that allows individuals to express their personal style. This approach merges functionality with fashion, providing customers with products that meet their practical needs while also enhancing their appearance.

In pursuit of this mission, the company is committed to maintaining **high ethical standards** in its production processes. This includes sourcing materials from sustainable suppliers, minimizing the environmental impact of manufacturing, and ensuring that workers involved in the production of the company's products are treated fairly and work in safe conditions. The company's long-term goal is to build a brand that is synonymous with both style and social responsibility, attracting customers who care about the ethical implications of their purchases.

The **global reach** of the company's e-commerce platform allows it to connect with customers from diverse backgrounds, making it a truly international brand. By offering shipping to various regions, including underserved markets, the company ensures that its high-quality eyewear is accessible to customers worldwide. Moreover, the platform's multilingual and currency-friendly features make it easy for customers to shop in their preferred language and currency, creating a seamless global shopping experience.

Market Demand Analysis (Market Share Definition)

A **market demand analysis** is essential for understanding the potential demand for a company's products or services. This process helps businesses evaluate the size of the market, identify customer needs, and determine their potential **market share**—the percentage of total sales in the market that the company can realistically capture. For the company focused on selling high-quality sunglasses and eyeglass frames, conducting a thorough market demand analysis allows it to estimate the total number of potential customers and project revenue based on the current trends in the eyewear industry. Market share can be defined through a combination of **quantitative** and **qualitative** factors:

- **Quantitative analysis** involves looking at existing market data, such as the total sales volume of sunglasses and eyeglass frames in key regions like North America, Europe, and Asia. For example, if the global eyewear market is valued at $100 billion, and the company aims to capture 0.5% of the market, this would translate to a potential market share of $500 million.
- **Qualitative analysis** focuses on consumer behavior, such as purchasing patterns, brand loyalty, and factors that influence buying decisions. For example, understanding that millennials and Gen Z consumers prioritize eco-friendly and stylish products can help the company tailor its offerings to meet those preferences.

By analyzing these factors, the company can better understand its **target audience**, segment the market based on demographics, and position its products to meet the specific needs of those segments. The goal of the market share analysis is to identify **growth opportunities** and align business strategies to capitalize on them. For example, if market trends indicate a growing demand for sustainable eyewear, the company can introduce eco-friendly sunglasses and frames to capture a larger share of that niche market.

Market Supply Analysis (Potential and Actual Competitors)

A **market supply analysis** focuses on identifying the **competitors** in the market and understanding their strengths, weaknesses, market position, and strategies. This analysis helps businesses anticipate competitive threats and carve out a unique position in the marketplace. For the company selling mid-to-high-end sunglasses and eyeglass frames, analyzing both **actual competitors** (those currently operating in the same space) and **potential competitors** (those who may enter the market) is essential for staying ahead of the competition.

Actual competitors include established brands in the eyewear industry that dominate the market, such as Ray-Ban, Oakley, and Warby Parker. These companies have strong brand recognition and established customer bases, making it challenging for new entrants to compete. However, the company can differentiate itself through niche strategies like offering unique designs, focusing on sustainability, or providing a superior online shopping experience. For example, by leveraging augmented reality (AR) tools that allow customers to try on glasses virtually, the company can provide a more personalized and engaging shopping experience than traditional competitors.

Potential competitors include startups or fashion brands that may decide to enter the eyewear market, especially as the demand for trendy, high-quality eyewear continues to grow. Monitoring **market trends** helps the company anticipate new entrants and adjust its product offerings or pricing strategies accordingly. For example, if a well-known fashion brand decides to launch its own line of sunglasses, the company may need to focus more on its eco-friendly materials or customization options to maintain its competitive edge.

Understanding **supply-side dynamics** also includes analyzing **supplier relationships** and the ability to scale production to meet growing demand. If competitors have exclusive relationships with certain manufacturers or access to lower production costs, it could impact the company's ability to compete on price or availability. Therefore, ensuring strong relationships with suppliers is key to maintaining a reliable and cost-effective supply chain.

Financial Plan: Drafting the Income Statement and Balance Sheet (to Determine Profit and/or Loss) and Reclassification into Key Performance Indicators (to Monitor Profitability, Solvency, Liquidity)

The **financial plan** is a vital part of business strategy, helping to determine the financial health and viability of the company. Drafting an **Income Statement** and **Balance Sheet** provides a clear picture of profitability, assets, liabilities, and equity. These financial documents are essential for making informed business decisions and securing investment from third-party funders. Additionally, reclassifying financial data into **Key Performance Indicators (KPIs)** helps monitor critical metrics such as **profitability**, **solvency**, and **liquidity**.

The **Income Statement** (or Profit and Loss Statement) summarizes the company's revenues and expenses over a given period, helping to calculate net income. Key components include:

- **Revenue**: Total sales from sunglasses and eyeglass frames.
- **Cost of Goods Sold (COGS)**: Direct costs associated with manufacturing the eyewear, including materials, labor, and production.
- **Operating Expenses**: Indirect costs such as marketing, salaries, rent, and administrative expenses.
- **Net Profit**: The company's total earnings after deducting COGS and operating expenses.

The **Balance Sheet** provides a snapshot of the company's financial standing at a specific point in time, showing:

- **Assets**: Including cash, inventory, accounts receivable, and property.
- **Liabilities**: Debt, accounts payable, and any other financial obligations.
- **Equity**: The value of the shareholders' stake in the company.

Once these statements are drafted, the next step is to **reclassify** them into **KPIs** that provide deeper insights into the company's financial health:

- **Profitability**: Calculated through **gross margin** and **net profit margin**, these metrics show how well the company is converting revenue into profit.
- **Solvency**: Monitored through the **debt-to-equity ratio**, which indicates the company's ability to meet long-term obligations.
- **Liquidity**: Measured by the **current ratio** and **quick ratio**, which assess the company's ability to cover short-term liabilities with current assets.

These KPIs offer management and investors a clear understanding of the company's financial performance and areas for improvement.

Financial Plan Presentation to Third-Party Funders

The **financial plan presentation** is a crucial tool for attracting third-party funders, such as venture capitalists, angel investors, or banks. This presentation highlights the company's financial viability, growth potential, and ability to generate returns on investment. A well-prepared financial plan not only showcases current performance but also outlines **projections** for future growth and profitability.

Key elements of the financial plan presentation include:

- **Executive Summary**: A brief overview of the company's business model, market opportunity, and financial health.
- **Income Statement Projections**: Detailing expected revenue growth, operating costs, and profit margins over the next 3 to 5 years. This gives investors a sense of the company's future profitability.
- **Cash Flow Forecasts**: Demonstrating the company's ability to manage cash effectively, ensuring that it can meet its obligations and reinvest in growth.
- **Balance Sheet Projections**: Showing how the company's assets, liabilities, and equity are expected to evolve over time.
- **Use of Funds**: Clearly outlining how the investment will be used, such as for product development, marketing, or international expansion.

- **Risk Analysis**: Highlighting potential challenges, such as competition or supply chain disruptions, and the strategies the company has in place to mitigate these risks.

This presentation needs to be **clear and compelling**, with visual aids such as charts, graphs, and key data points to help funders quickly understand the company's financial outlook and potential for returns. Investors are particularly interested in metrics like **ROI (Return on Investment)**, which demonstrates how their capital will be used and the expected financial returns over time.

Supplier Analysis and Product Selection (for Us: 3 Sunglasses Lines and 3 Types of Eyeglass Frames for Men and the Same for Women)

Conducting a thorough **supplier analysis** is a key factor in ensuring the company's success, especially when focusing on high-quality sunglasses and eyeglass frames. The right suppliers provide products that meet the company's standards for durability, design, and sustainability while offering competitive pricing and reliable delivery. Supplier analysis involves evaluating potential suppliers based on criteria such as **cost**, **quality control**, **manufacturing capabilities**, and **lead times**. Building strong partnerships with these suppliers ensures a consistent and efficient supply chain, helping the company deliver products that meet customer expectations.

For the company's product offerings, careful **product selection** is essential to cater to the diverse preferences of the target market. The company will launch **three lines of sunglasses** and **three types of eyeglass frames** for both men and women, ensuring a broad range of styles and functionalities that appeal to various customer segments.

Sunglasses Lines:
1. **Classic Line**:
2. Targeting consumers who appreciate timeless, elegant designs, the Classic Line will feature universally loved styles such as aviators, wayfarers, and square frames.
    - Materials like stainless steel, acetate, and polarized lenses will be used to provide durability and UV protection.
    - Ideal for customers who value both fashion and function in their everyday eyewear.

3. **Fashion Line**:
   - This line will cater to trend-conscious customers looking for bold, statement-making sunglasses. The frames will include oversized designs, cat-eye shapes, and a variety of vibrant colors and patterns.
   - Designed with fashion-forward customers in mind, the Fashion Line will prioritize aesthetics without compromising on quality.
4. **Sports/Outdoor Line**:
   - Aimed at active customers, this line will focus on performance eyewear. Sunglasses in this category will feature lightweight, flexible frames with polarized lenses designed for outdoor activities such as hiking, running, and cycling.
   - Emphasis will be placed on functionality, with lenses offering enhanced UV protection, anti-glare coatings, and impact resistance.

Eyeglass Frames for Men and Women:

1. **Professional Line**:
   - This line will offer minimalist, elegant designs that are ideal for workplace and formal environments. Frames will be made from durable materials like titanium and high-grade plastics to provide long-lasting comfort for daily wear.
   - The focus will be on sleek, neutral-colored frames that appeal to professionals looking for subtle yet sophisticated eyewear.
2. **Trendy Line**:
   - The Trendy Line will target younger, fashion-conscious consumers who see eyeglasses as a fashion accessory. Frames will be available in bold shapes and eye-catching colors, designed to complement various personal styles.

- This line will include playful and contemporary designs, appealing to customers who want their eyewear to reflect their individuality.
3. **Eco-Friendly Line**:
    - Reflecting the company's commitment to sustainability, the Eco-Friendly Line will use environmentally conscious materials like recycled plastics and bamboo. These frames will appeal to consumers who prioritize ethical and eco-friendly products.
    - This line will highlight the company's mission to combine style with responsibility, ensuring that fashion and environmental stewardship go hand-in-hand.

Each product line will include a balance of aesthetic appeal, comfort, and functionality, ensuring the company can serve various segments of its target market while maintaining high standards of quality and sustainability.

Pricing Model

An effective **pricing model** is essential for achieving profitability while remaining competitive in the market. For a company positioned in the mid-to-high price range, pricing must reflect the quality of the materials and craftsmanship involved, while also being attractive to target consumers who are willing to pay a premium for stylish and durable eyewear. The pricing model will be developed based on several factors, including **cost of production**, **competitor pricing**, and the perceived value of the product.

Key considerations for the pricing model include:

- **Cost of Goods Sold (COGS)**: This includes all direct costs associated with the production of the sunglasses and eyeglass frames, such as raw materials, manufacturing, and shipping. These costs form the base upon which the pricing structure will be built.
- **Perceived Value**: Since the company is targeting customers who are willing to pay more for high-quality, fashionable products, the pricing must reflect the **brand positioning** as a premium offering. By emphasizing the craftsmanship, materials, and durability of the products, the company can justify higher price points.
- **Market Demand**: Pricing will also be adjusted based on customer demand. In high-demand markets, such as North America and Europe, pricing may reflect the willingness of consumers to pay for premium eyewear.

The company will aim to maintain a balance between offering affordable luxury and ensuring sufficient margins to sustain operations and growth.

Mark-Up

The **mark-up** is the percentage added to the **cost of goods sold** (COGS) to determine the selling price, ensuring the company achieves profitability. Given the mid-to-high-end positioning of the company, the mark-up will reflect both the premium quality of the products and the need to cover operational costs, marketing efforts, and customer service.

In the eyewear industry, typical mark-up rates range from **2.5x to 4x** the production cost, depending on the brand's positioning. For the company's sunglasses and eyeglass frames:

- **Sunglasses** will have a higher mark-up due to the value placed on design and UV protection features. For example, a pair of sunglasses with a COGS of $50 may be sold at $150, applying a **3x mark-up**.
- **Eyeglass frames** will have a slightly lower mark-up, particularly for professional and eco-friendly lines, to remain accessible to a broader customer base. A frame with a production cost of $40 may be priced at $100, applying a **2.5x mark-up**.

This pricing strategy will allow the company to cover production costs while generating sufficient profit margins to support growth, marketing, and operational expenses.

Additionally, by keeping mark-ups competitive within the industry standard, the company can position itself as offering **high-quality, stylish eyewear** at fair prices, further boosting customer loyalty and brand perception.

Marketing Plan (Online Advertising) and Social Media Channels

A robust **marketing plan** will be key to the company's success, leveraging **online advertising** and **social media channels** to drive brand awareness, engage customers, and increase sales. Given the company's e-commerce platform, the marketing focus will be on digital channels to reach a global audience and build a strong online presence.

Online Advertising:
- **Google Ads**: The company will use **Google Ads** to target specific keywords related to sunglasses, eyeglasses, and eyewear fashion trends. By utilizing pay-per-click (PPC) advertising, the company can ensure that its ads appear at the top of search results when potential customers are actively looking for premium eyewear. This approach allows for highly targeted campaigns, improving return on ad spend (ROAS).
- **Facebook and Instagram Ads**: Visual platforms like **Facebook** and **Instagram** are ideal for showcasing the company's stylish products through image-driven ads. These ads can target specific demographics, such as fashion-conscious consumers aged 25–45, who are more likely to purchase high-end eyewear. Additionally, Instagram's **shopping feature** allows customers to purchase directly through the platform, streamlining the buying process.

- **Retargeting Campaigns**: The company will implement retargeting campaigns for customers who have visited the website but did not make a purchase. By showing personalized ads to these customers across various platforms, the company can encourage them to return and complete their purchase.

Social Media Channels:
- **Instagram**: Given the highly visual nature of the eyewear industry, Instagram will be the primary social media platform for the company. It allows for high-quality images and videos of the company's products, along with influencer collaborations, user-generated content, and customer reviews. Instagram's **Stories** and **Reels** features will be utilized to engage customers and showcase product launches and behind-the-scenes content.
- **Facebook**: As a platform with a broad demographic reach, Facebook will be used to promote brand awareness and customer engagement through posts, contests, and community-building efforts. The company will also use **Facebook Ads** to reach specific target audiences and promote special deals or new product lines.
- **Pinterest**: Pinterest is ideal for showcasing style inspiration, mood boards, and fashion trends that feature the company's sunglasses and eyeglass frames. Users often browse Pinterest for fashion ideas, making it a key platform for driving organic traffic to the company's e-commerce site.

Made in the USA
Middletown, DE
11 November 2024